COLLECTORS' BLUE BOOKS

Chinese Blue and White

ANN FRANK

STUDIO VISTA, LONDON

FRONTISPIECE: Ming peasant jar with dragon in "finger painting" style. Freer Gallery of Art, Washington, D.C.

FARNHAM SCHOOL OF ART

SBN 289 79735 7

Published in London 1970 by Studio Vista Ltd, Blue Star House, Highgate Hill, London N19

Printed in the United States of America
Jacket designed by the Bert Clarke Design Group
Book designed by Joseph Bourke Del Valle

Chinese Blue and White

洪武
年製

Hung Wu (1368–1398)

Yung Lo (1403–1424)

永樂
年製

Yung Lo (1403–1424)

大明宣
德年製

Hsüan Te (1426–1435)

大明成
化年製

Ch'êng Hua (1465–1487)

大明弘
治年製

Hung Chih (1485–1505)

大明正
德年製

Cheng Te (1506–1521)

大明嘉
靖年製

Chia Ching (1522–1566)

大明隆
慶年製

Lung Ch'ing (1567–1572)

大明萬
曆年製

Wan Li (1573–1619)

大明天
啟年製

T'ien Ch'i (1621–1627)

崇禎
年製

Ch'ung Chêng (1628–1643)

Note: Sung Dynasty (960–1279)   Yüan Dynasty (1280–1368)

大清順治年製

Shun Chih (1644-1661)

大清康熙年製

K'ang Hsi (1662-1722)

大清雍正年製

Yung Cheng (1723-1735)

大清乾隆年製

Ch'ien Lung (1736-1795)

嘉慶年製

Chia Ch'ing (1796-1820)

大清道光年製

Tao Kuang (1821-1850)

大清咸豐年製

Hsien Fêng (1851-1861)

大清同治年製

T'ung Chih (1862-1873)

大清光緒年製

Kuang Hsü (1874-1908)

大清宣統年製

Hsüan T'ung (1909-1912)

Early 15th century plate with lotus scroll and borders of mixed floral scroll and waves. Courtesy Frank Caro, New York.

CHAPTER I

The Manufacture of Blue and White

BLUE AND WHITE, of all Chinese ceramics, has enjoyed the most universal and long-lived popularity. Its many styles seem to sum up Chinese design. During the entire period of manufacture of Blue and White, Ch'ing-tê Chên in Kiangsi province was the center of the Chinese porcelain industry. Porcelain is the only product of Ch'ing-tê Chên; but the town has stocked a world of pantries, and at times encompassed an enormous worker population, in the eighteenth century outnumbering all the cities of the world save Constantinople. Throughout the Ming and Ch'ing dynasties the workshops, with the exception of the state-run Imperial factory, were commercial, capitalistic ventures. Each factory made a variety of kinds and qualities of wares, both for the domestic market and for export. Pattern books were used, and division of labor was practiced in all but the smallest shops; both factors contributed to a standardization of styles and qualities. In the Imperial factory, work was so minutely parceled that one man painted the blue ring near the lip of cups and bowls, another painted reign marks, another drew outlines of landscapes, and another laid in washes. Each had his own specialty, and a finished cup was the sum of many men's skills.

Separately owned kilns were rented by workshops when they were ready to fire their wares; and itinerant work gangs were hired to stoke the furnaces with brushwood. Each firing took several days, because a temperature of 1500°C was required to vitrify the clay and turn it to porcelain. Then the kiln had to cool before the wares could be removed. In present-day China the potteries are all state-owned, and are run by committees consisting of workers, "old cadres," and a representative of the local army. Continuously functioning kilns have been installed that use coal, gas or diesel oil.

Kaolin, the chief ingredient of the porcelain body, was mined in the Ma

Ts'ang Mountains, and after that source gave out in the reign of Chia Ching, at Kimun in Anhwei province. The kaolinic rock was ground, washed and molded into bricks near the site of the mines, then shipped to Ch'ing-tê Chên. There the bricks were sold to the potting factories, reground and prepared for use. Much the same process was applied to petuntse (the name is derived from *pai tun tzu,* "little white bricks"), which was mined in the Kaoling Mountains near Ch'ing-tê Chên.[1] Petuntse is the basis of glaze material, and is added to kaolin to make a vitrifiable body substance. Both rocks are varieties of feldspar.

When heated, kaolin remains white and refractory, whereas petuntse becomes colorless and glassy; but traces of iron oxide in either material can result in discoloration during firing. If there is a reducing atmosphere in the kiln, that is, if little air is allowed to enter the kiln and few oxygen atoms are present in the atmosphere, the oxygen is sucked from the iron oxide, leaving the iron in the glaze to show a greenish hue. If there is an oxidizing atmosphere (air flowing freely into the kiln, with readily available oxygen atoms) the iron will obtain oxygen atoms, tinting glazed areas creamy and the exposed portions of the porcelain body rust color. Frequently porcelains are seen with greenish glazes but with patches of the exposed biscuit of footrims colored orange. In such cases the firing atmosphere was a reducing one, but the body material was still hot and subject to further chemical change when the kiln door was opened, although the glaze surface had cooled and hardened sufficiently to be impenetrable to oxygen atoms. The draft of air admitted oxygen to the still susceptible iron on the hot surface of the unglazed biscuit, producing a visible coating of iron oxide.

Cobalt, which appears gray before firing, is painted directly onto the unfired, unglazed pottery body. The entire object is then either dipped in glaze or sprayed with glaze blown through a gauze-covered bamboo tube. As the glaze dries, it becomes opaque, obliterating the painted decoration beneath. In the kiln the glaze is clarified and the cobalt turns blue. Since Blue and White requires only one firing, it has always been one of the most economical of decorated porcelains to manufacture.

---

[1] Père d'Entrecolles, in his description of porcelain manufacture, gave these materials the names by which we know them; unfortunately he thought that kaolin, not petuntse, came from the Kaoling Mountains. Bushell, *Oriental Ceramic Art.*

Chia Ching *kuan* jar with *wa wa* motif. Freer Gallery of Art, Washington, D.C.

14th century *kuan* jar with aquatic scene of carp, water weeds and sprouting lotuses; wave border at lip. Courtesy of The Brooklyn Museum.

CHAPTER II

The History of Blue and White

COBALT WAS USED TO DECORATE ORIENTAL pottery as early as the T'ang dynasty (A.D. 618–907), but no way was known to keep the color from spreading and dripping when it was heated, even in the gentle earthenware kiln. Its use on the high-fired porcelains of the period—the creamy Ting ware, the icy Hsing and the watery-blue glazed Ch'ing Pai—was not attempted. In the early part of the Yüan dynasty, the potters of Ch'ing-tê Chên began to experiment with underglaze painting. But their rough products were only moderately successful, and it was not until the fourteenth century, when Persian cobalt was exported to China, that a pigment stable enough to hold its design was available.

Trade among China, the Middle East and Europe had been carried on intermittently from prehistoric times. But since the fall of the T'ang dynasty the great steppe of Turkestan, which forms a natural causeway between China and the West, had been inhabited by hostile nomadic tribes; and direct communication was cut off. In the thirteenth century a Mongol tribe of the steppe, under the leadership of Genghis Khan, began the bloody program of conquest that ultimately resulted in the unification of China, Turkestan and the Middle East under a single rule, and the reopening of overland trade. By the late thirteenth century, when Marco Polo and Friar William of Rubruck visited the Orient, the first Persian cobalt was being used experimentally in Chinese workshops, and a well-controlled medium for painting on porcelain was being devised. The medium offered opportunities that released a spate of decorative creativity. Busy designs covered every kind of object, contrasting sharply with the cool monochromes of the celadons just then passing out of vogue.

The popularity of Blue and White spread to the Middle East, where collections of the ware were amassed by the nobility. Kings exchanged presents of porcelain, and a dish was a suitable reward for a general. In 1611 Shah Abbās, the ruler of Iran, made a gift of his collection to the shrine of his saintly ancestor Ishaq Safi ed-Din at Ardebil. Arab sea trade took Blue and White to southeast Asia, India, the Philippines, Indonesia and even, indirectly, to Europe. At once, the porcelain was treasured by the head-taking tribes of the Pacific and by the Elizabethan court.

With the fall of the Mongol Yüan dynasty in 1368 and the establishment of the native Ming court, royal favor gave Blue and White the honor of highest approval. The first Ming emperor, Hung Wu, instituted the Imperial porcelain factory at Ch'ing-tê Chên, which proceeded to make Blue and White, underglaze red and plain white porcelains for the exclusive use of the court. It was on these wares that the first reign marks (*nien hao*)[2] were used with any consistency. Thus Blue and White is one of the oldest porcelains that can be attributed to specific reigns with accuracy. Underglaze red was used only occasionally after the early Ming period, and white ware was made chiefly for times of mourning; so Blue and White has the longest period of continuous manufacture of any porcelain that can be precisely identified. These factors partly account for the favoritism it has enjoyed among scholarly collectors.

Decorative styles became more sober with the advent of the Ming, but the vitality of the young technique was not a bit impaired. Patterns of traditional brocades were adapted to the sculptural surface with deceptive ease. Later the surest signs of decadence would appear in the failure to make these motifs, borrowed from another medium, fit the ceramic form without looking stilted.

Persian cobalt ceased to arrive by the overland route as soon as the Mongol Empire fell, but an alternative source of supply was soon found. The third Ming emperor, Yung Lo, sent a fleet of military junks on a series of expeditions through the South China Sea, the Indian Ocean, the Persian Gulf, and into the Red Sea. Under the admiralship of Cheng Ho, a court eunuch of unparalleled abilities as a navigator, soldier and diplomat, the fleet inspired such awe in all the countries it visited that embassies bearing tribute arrived in Peking regu-

---

[2] In the Ming and Ch'ing dynasties the period of an emperor's reign was given an auspicious name. Through use, the name came to refer to the emperor himself. Names of dynasties are similarly auspicious and have nothing to do with the family name of the ruling house. This does not hold true for dynasties prior to the Yüan, however; then there could be several different reign periods within a single emperor's rule; and dynastic names were associated with the region that the ruling house had dominated before rising to the throne.

larly for decades to come. Sumatran ambassadors brought presents of a fine cobalt, which was found to be as well suited to porcelain as the Persian color. The new pigment was called *su-ma-li* or *su-ma-ni* blue, to differentiate it from *hui hui ch'ing* (Muhammadan blue); but there is little difference in appearance between the two imported pigments.

Chinese interest in maritime exploits waned after the death of Yung Lo; but the impression left by Cheng Ho and his well-armed ships lasted until the reign of Ch'êng Hua. By then Sumatra, busy with her own internal affairs, no longer felt the need to send tribute to Peking; the potters of Ch'ing-tê Chên had to learn to refine and control their native color. From that time until the end of the reign of Chêng Tê the events of history dictated the fashion in porcelain, but not a change in materials or markets. Ch'êng Hua was much influenced by the Lady Wen, and delicate tablewares of feminine appeal were preferred. Chêng Tê favored the Muslim community; shapes derived from Middle Eastern vessels appeared in abundance; and the Muhammadan scroll became a popular decorative motif.

In 1516 the first European ship, commanded by the Portuguese captain Perestrello, sailed up the Pearl River to Canton. This expedition was greeted by the Chinese with the same civility and businesslike procedure the Celestial Kingdom accorded the familiar Arab trade. The Europeans did their business and departed without incident. The following year a Portuguese fleet, under Fernao Peres de Andrade, also found commercial success at Canton, despite a

Chêng Tê pen rest in stylized mountain shape. Thick glaze blurs the *ju-i* scroll decoration and the label, which reads "pen rest." The Metropolitan Museum of Art, New York, Rogers Fund, 1917.

misunderstanding at the outset, when the ships fired a salvo that the Chinese mistook for an attack.

The felicitous beginning of trade with the West did not last long. For it was not only commerce that moved the Iberians, but also a fervent desire to convert the "infidels of the East" to Christianity, combined with an attitude that the world was theirs for the taking. Conversion was accomplished by force where persuasion failed, and heathens' claims to life and property were little regarded. The ports along the Eastern trade route where the Portuguese had murdered and pillaged were visited by Arab merchants, and news of the foreigners' crimes spread to Peking. When, in 1518, Simão Peres de Andrade, whose ships followed his brother's to Canton, committed piracy in the Pearl River, he was driven out of Chinese waters and all ports were officially closed to Europeans.

By smuggling and plundering, Portugal continued to obtain Chinese goods, and porcelains were among the most sought-after items. But it was not until 1557, when her sailors occupied the island of Macao at the mouth of the Pearl River, that a regular Portuguese trade was established. China permitted the taking of Macao for the sake of a profitable business and a new source of taxes; but the foreigners were allowed to travel up the river to the port city only twice a year. There they were confined to the wharves and the adjacent suburb, but they could make purchases in the shops and leave orders to be filled for the next biannual trip. Quantities of Blue and White reached Europe through this trade. Many porcelains were made to European specifications, some with inscriptions in badly misunderstood Portuguese.

During the reigns of Chia Ching, Lung Ch'ing and Wan Li, Portugal preyed upon Arab shipping and gradually built a monopoly of Eastern trade. But China was too concerned with the problems of incursions from Mongolia and Japan to bother much about the change of power at sea. Chia Ching disliked the Arabs and removed from office all those whom his father had favored. Not surprisingly, Middle Eastern influence vanished from the potteries as quickly as from the court. Taoist motifs and the traditional brocades took the place of the Muhammadan scrolls. During this period the quality of porcelains decreased, but this cannot be blamed on the growing conservatism. The wars

Chia Ching double-gourd vase with *Shou* and *ju-i* sprays sprouting from behind rock on upper bulb, and scene of the Three Friends and symbolic animals on lower bulb. The British Museum, London.

China sustained to hold her borders against nomadic invaders from the north and the harrying Japanese depleted her revenues; little was left for the Imperial factory. Nevertheless, the court needed enormous quantities of porcelain, so quality had to be sacrificed. Blue and White took on the stilted look of mass production. In retrospect the most cheering development of the late Ming period seems to have taken place in the poorer commercial factories, which neither were under the pressure of heavy orders from the court nor sought to imitate the Imperial products. There a freer decorative style and a more fanciful range of subjects were introduced.

Until the beginning of the seventeenth century Portugal maintained her hold on Far Eastern commerce. Spain (which had explored the Americas, sailed across the Pacific and colonized the Philippine Islands) obtained a relatively small quantity of Chinese goods from the China-Philippine trade. The other countries of Europe bought their silks, spices and porcelains in Lisbon. But in 1595 Philip II closed Lisbon to English and Dutch shipping and entered upon a politico-religious war against those Protestant countries. Dutch and English merchants responded by forming East India trading companies and sailing to the Orient themselves, plundering any Portuguese ships they met along the way. Neither company undertook a voyage to China immediately, however.

In 1603 a decisive event occurred when Dutch privateers captured the Portuguese caraak *Santa Caterina* in the Strait of Malacca. Her cargo, which was entirely of the cheapest commercial Blue and White porcelain, achieved such high prices at auction on the wharves of Amsterdam that Dutch mercants promptly saw the value of opening a regular trade with China.

The following year the first Dutch vessel arrived at the mouth of the Pearl River. But trade was not to be so easily accomplished. Guns on Macao kept the Dutch from entering the river, while the Portuguese warned the officials of Canton not to trade with the newcomers.

China kept her ports closed. But Dutch ships remained in the East, obtaining Chinese products through privateering and smuggling along the southern coast. In 1624 a Dutch colony was established on Formosa. Fourteen years later Holland won exclusive right to trade with Japan and establish trading posts, first at Hirado and then at Deshima, an island in the harbor of Nagasaki. Through these ports quantities of Blue and White, similar to that sold from the caraak *Santa Caterina,* were sent to Holland as *kraakporselein.*

The English East India Company, though it was founded in 1600, two years before its Dutch counterpart, was slower to send a ship to China. The first English ships to reach Canton were not of the Company, but of the Courteen Association, a joint-stock company. The four ships were denied permission to anchor and carry out trade, again on the advice of the Portuguese. In frustration, the English captain fired his cannon at a Chinese fortification, and confirmed the Chinese in their determination not to trade with Britain. English ships joined the Dutch in the surreptitious trade along the coast.

The Chinese, with reason, looked upon all Westerners as barbarians, calling them *yang kuei,* "foreign devils." The Europeans' acts of piracy and privateering and their disregard of the laws and customs of the lands they visited seemed to prove that they were indeed a people without civilization. As long as the Ming held control, trade other than the concession granted to Portugal

K'ang Hsi teapot with "Long Elizas" and potted peonies on raised petal-shaped panels. European mount. The Metropolitan Museum of Art, New York.

K'ang Hsi plate with historical scene and brocade border with petal reserves. Courtesy Mr. and Mrs. Carroll L. Cartwright.

was refused. But by the end of the reign of Wan Li central power was dissolving, weakened by wars with Japan, internal mismanagement and civil rebellion. The government lacked the means, if not the inclination, to curb the ever-growing illegal trade. Orders for porcelains in European shapes were filled at Ch'ing-tê Chên without intervention. The potters found in the export trade a replacement for the domestic market, which was dwindling because of the unsure economy of the times. Imperial potters out of employment set up their own shops and made ceramics to European order. But for the most part the craftsmen were left to their own inspiration, and there were many innovations in forms and decorations.

During the reigns of T'ien Ch'i and Ch'ung Chêng the Imperial factory seems to have been closed entirely. Clearly the finest craftsmanship was expended on the commercial wares, many of which reached Europe. The few pieces that bear reign marks and may have been intended for the palace are roughly potted and their designs are sketchy. The easy-looking draftsmanship used on wares for the Japanese market added a new, flowing quality to figure drawing; figures and landscapes superseded the old brocades in popularity.

The Imperial factory stagnated until the second reign of the Ch'ing. In the interim the Ming dynasty fell and Li Tzu-ch'êng, the leader of the most powerful of several guerrilla bands, proclaimed himself first emperor of the Shun dynasty. By 1644 the overthrow of the old ruling house was completed. The last Ming emperor had committed suicide as Li's army entered Peking, and there was little opposition in the provinces. But a disastrous personal dispute arose between Li and General Wu San-kuei,[3] whose troops guarded the eastern gate of the Great Wall against attempted incursions from the Mongolian Manchu kingdom in the north.

The Mongols, after having been driven out of China by the Ming, remained in the northeast region beyond the Wall. At first they returned to their ancient nomadic way of life, roaming the country in small tribes, but in 1618 a chief named Nurhachu formed the tribes into the Manchu kingdom, and adopted a policy of expansion into Chinese territory. At the time of the fall of the Ming, the kingdom had spread as far south as the Great Wall. But because a regency ruled the country, acting for a child king, the greater military effort of extending the kingdom beyond the Wall had been temporarily suspended.

---

[3] Li refused to return a singing girl whom Wu San-kuei claimed belonged to his harem.

Wu San-kuei appealed to the Mongols, offering to open the gates of the Wall if they would help to avenge the Ming and drive Li Tzu-ch'êng from the throne. The combined forces of Wu and the Manchu defeated the Shun army and sent them in full retreat to the western provinces. Wu followed, bent on revenge, and the Manchu were left to occupy Peking, unopposed. In 1644 the Mongolian child king was proclaimed first emperor of the new Ch'ing dynasty. For thirty years the southern provinces rebelled in support of a surviving Ming prince, but eventually, under the second Ch'ing, K'ang Hsi, Manchu rule prevailed and China entered a long period of peaceful but humiliating foreign rule.

Because of the disorders in the south, little was done to revive the Imperial porcelain factory until the reign of K'ang Hsi was well established, though records of orders sent from the court during the first Ch'ing reign do exist. K'ang Hsi was an energetic patron of the arts as well as a wise and strong ruler; and his interest led him to attempt to move all the Imperial workshops onto the palace grounds. This plan proved undesirable for porcelain manufacture; so in 1683 the factory in Ch'ing-tê Chên was reopened. The free style of the commercial potters of the Transitional period (1627–1683) was refined, and much excellent Blue and White was produced. More innovations in design appeared than ever before, and control of the native pigment achieved new heights of perfection.

In 1699 K'ang Hsi opened the port of Canton to a restricted but legally sanctioned foreign trade. The countries of Europe were allowed to conduct business and to build their own warehouses, called Hongs, on the docks. Purchases of tea, silk and commercial-quality porcelain could be made in the shops contiguous to the docks; but foreigners were neither permitted to travel through China nor to learn the language. To the Chinese mind Europeans remained barbarians; and the Manchus, who were themselves susceptible to that epithet, were not inclined to champion the "foreign devils."

Chinese middlemen, called Hong merchants, were appointed to fill the orders for the European trade; they were also held responsible for the conduct of the Europeans in Canton. Although their business was highly lucrative, the Hong merchants lacked prestige among their countrymen, and their liability for the behavior of foreign sailors placed them in constant legal peril. Nevertheless they seem to have been very honorable men; some were so popular with the Westerners with whom they dealt that ships and blends of tea were named for them. But the positive aspects of the China trade were all but outweighed by the negative. Tribute, as well as graft and heavy port duties, was extracted from the foreign traders. Europeans found the notion of tribute especially irksome. To them China was a curiosity, a land of well-mannered, industrious heathens, not at all the awe-inspiring fountainhead of universal culture which she was accustomed to consider herself. Western animosity grew, aggravated by Chinese refusal to deal with the fast-developing countries of Europe as cultural equals, and bruised by the economic pressure of having to pay in bullion for everything bought. There was little the West had to offer that the Chinese wanted in exchange for their own products, save gold or silver.

Hong merchants were not the only mediators between East and West during the early years of the eighteenth century, however. French Jesuit missionaries were well received at court and became both popular and influential. The

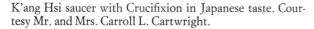

K'ang Hsi saucer with Crucifixion in Japanese taste. Courtesy Mr. and Mrs. Carroll L. Cartwright.

Jesuits were ideally equipped to impress Chinese scholars with the civilized nature of the West; and the Fathers introduced several of the discoveries of Occidental science and technology to the court. In reverse, the letters that they sent home provided the foundation of the eighteenth-century European notion of China. For a while Jesuits were allowed to set up missions in provincial towns and to convert the population to Christianity. One of these missionaries, Père d'Entrecolles, had the unique opportunity to live in Ch'ing-tê Chên. His letters, dated 1712 and 1722, explain the process of porcelain manufacture, and are the earliest European source on the subject.

At the end of the reign of K'ang Hsi the Jesuits lost favor, and a promising beginning of understanding was cut short. Conservatism grew as the dynasty became thoroughly settled. The Manchus obscured their foreignness by identifying themselves with the Chinese past. For Blue and White this meant a return to the traditional patterns of the fifteenth century, but in a manner so reverential as to be stifling.

The reigns of Yung Chêng and Ch'ien Lung were prosperous, but not so wisely governed as that of K'ang Hsi. Opposition to alien rule increased; and the repressive measures ordered by the Ch'ing became gradually less effective. At the end of the reign of Ch'ien Lung rebellion in the countryside was coupled with subversive activities on the part of European powers, which were not content with Chinese policies of trade. Through the early nineteenth century the Ch'ing remained intransigent both in domestic and in foreign affairs, arousing ever-stronger opposition. Their refusal to negotiate new trade agreements so angered the British that war became inevitable. But the Chinese court remained unconcerned at growing British naval strength, and the spectacle of British imperialism in India did not alert them.

The year 1839 saw the beginning of the Opium Wars. The English were victorious after three years of sporadic struggle, obtaining considerable trade concessions, which were soon shared by the United States, France, Belgium and Sweden. But the agreements were not satisfactory to either side, and war again broke out. New treaties, more demanding than before, were extracted from China. When the court reneged and met Western diplomats with troops, the war was again renewed. British soldiers looted the summer palace, Yuan Ming Yuan, and burned it to the ground in retaliation for the emperor's bad faith. Some of the first Imperial porcelains to reach the West arrived as booty from this adventure.

Ch'ien Lung four-legged teapot *(ho)* decorated in Hsüan Te style with false "heaped-and-piled" effect. Museum of Fine Arts, Boston, John Gardner Coolidge Collection.

While European dissatisfaction was becoming bellicose, domestic unrest was also igniting. The rebellion of the White Lotus sect in the late eighteenth century was followed by the rise of numerous other secret revolutionary societies. In 1850 a protracted war began in which the T'ai Ping rebels, a militant Christian sect that followed the vision of its own prophet, conquered much of southern China. Lack of organization on the part of the rebels, not the strength of the Ch'ing government, kept the T'ai Ping from taking Peking.

The effect of these disorders on the porcelain industry was catastrophic. The elegant but uninspired products of the early Ch'ien Lung period had been imitated with gradually decreasing care. Then, in 1853 the T'ai Ping rebels destroyed Ch'ing-tê Chên, and the population of the town was murdered or dispersed. Years of continuity in work are required for an apprentice to develop master skills; but without masters to learn from, the old craft methods may be permanently lost. Although Ch'ing-tê Chên was rebuilt in 1864, the skills of the lost potters did not revive. A brief renaissance occurred at the end of the nineteenth century, during the reign of Kuang Hsü, for the Empress Dowager Tzu Hsi was a patroness of the craft. But Blue and White gained no benefit, for enamel wares were her chief concern.

In recent years, under communism, Ch'ing-tê Chên has entered a new phase, guided, from all appearances, by the commercial success of the Japanese porcelain industry. Cheap tablewares, adorned with stenciled or transfer decorations, are the staples; but some excellent copies of Sung celadons and Ming Blue and White are also made.

ABOVE: Early Yüan stem cup with chrysanthemum scroll (see page 29). The British Museum, London.
OPPOSITE: Late 14th–early 15th century covered *mei p'ing* with Taoist landscape, classic scroll, lotus scroll, cash pattern, and false gadroons. Museum of Fine Arts, Boston, Clara Bertram Kimball Collection.

Hung Chih plate with the five-petaled flower motif of the Imperial table service.
Background filled in with yellow enamel. The Metropolitan Museum of Art, New
York, Rogers Fund, 1919.

CHAPTER III

Styles of Blue and White

The Yüan Dynasty and Ming Hung Wu

SURVIVING BLUE AND WHITE made during the Yüan rule may be divided into two distinct groups. The first is roughly formed, and shows similarities to provincial manufactures and to Shou Fu ware, a descendant of Ch'ing Pai. Typical Shou Fu dragons or floral scrolls are sometimes drawn in slip[4] in low relief beneath the glaze, augmenting the painted decoration. The body is crisp and is grayish or milky in tone; the blue pigment is blackish or gray. Bowls, stem cups, incense burners, small jars, and pairs of vases in a variety of shapes are encountered. Most have freely drawn, sketchy decorations of twining, daisylike chrysanthemum scrolls, lotus sprays, or exuberant dragons with long, snaky necks. "Flaming pearls" and classic scrolls appear in a swift, calligraphic style, more suggestive of an unknown script than of the traditional subjects they represent. Cups and bowls are thin-walled, but vases are heavily built, and usually sport ornate handles hung with loops. The thick glaze rounds and gives a softened look to elaborate shapes. Where the glaze gathers in crevices, a deepening blue tone is perceptible.

A far more sophisticated fourteenth-century porcelain, for the most part of slightly later manufacture, is that familiar from the Middle Eastern collections. These pieces are heavily constructed, and there is Persian influence in many of the shapes. The array preserved for us includes large plates with plain or foliate rims; bowls with plain, foliate or inturned rims; and ewers, cup stands, rectangular pilgrim bottles, *mei p'ing*,[5] *kuan* jars and large octagonal double-gourd vases. Plates are most common, however.

[4] Diluted clay.
[5] A wine jar used to hold a branch of flowering *Prunus* (*mei*).

LEFT: Yüan vase with lotus scroll, stiff leaf borders on neck, and *ju-i* head scroll at foot. The Metropolitan Museum of Art, New York, Rogers Fund, 1922.

RIGHT: 14th century pear bottle with cloud-shaped cartouches containing scalloped waves and a lotus alternating with "flaming pearls"; bands of stiff leaves, key fret, false gadroons, and classic scroll: elements of both rough and export ware. Museum of Fine Arts, Boston, Clara Bertram Kimball Collection.

The many motifs for concentric borders and central decorations are adaptations of traditional brocades. Scrolls of crapemyrtle and blackberry lily, lozenge diapers, waves with heavily outlined crests and thumbprintlike swells, floral sprays or classic scrolls are seen in narrow bands or on the rims of almost every piece. Among the patterns for wider bands and cavettos are lotus, peony and chrysanthemum scrolls (in the usual blue on white or in white reserved on a blue-washed ground—sometimes the white is accented by molded low relief), stiff leaves, and false gadroons containing scrolls, lotuses, flaming pearls or symbolic objects. Central motifs depict aquatic scenes with fish and underwater plants (a rhebus meaning abundance); ponds with Mandarin ducks (symbolic of marital happiness); phoenixes flying over flowers; dragons amid flames or clouds; clusters of fruit; or rock gardens with melons, plantain trees, bamboos, morning glories and grape vines. Cartouches sometimes augment the bands, dividing space farther so that more patterns can be combined. Some designs such as scalloped waves with flowers, horses or conch shells superimposed on them appear primarily as filling for cartouches.

Fourteenth-century Blue and White lacks reign marks, but a magnificent pair of vases in the Percival David collection bears a date mark corresponding to the year 1351. These have provided the major clue for identifying contemporary porcelains, for it is a rare piece that does not share at least one of the eight motifs displayed on the David vases.

Bases of virtually all known fourteenth-century porcelains are unglazed, and the footrings are of heavy construction. Firing has oxidized the iron in the exposed biscuit, turning it a soft apricot color. The cobalt was not perfectly ground, and the painter's brush often deposited flakes and chunks of pigment in the drawing, producing to varying degrees the "heaped-and-piled" effect for which early-fifteenth-century wares are famous. The "heaps" are intense, blackish specks and blotches of irregular shape; they may break the surface of the glaze, causing brownish-black burned spots. The cobalt itself shows a blackish sapphire tone, and the white ground is often bluish or gray. The glaze has a dense, fine pitting, with a "fatlike" texture.

At the Ottoman court of Suleiman I (the Magnificent) the cumbersome serving plates and bowls were provided with silver covers and were carried from the kitchens to the royal presence by the head taster and his assistants. There they were set on rugs which had been covered over with a tablecloth. Small

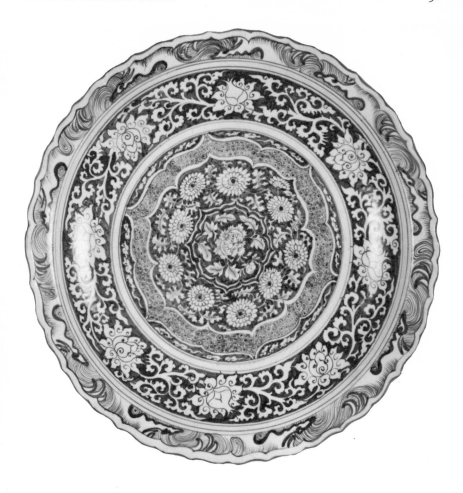

14th century plate with foliate rim, decoration reserved in white on blue. The British Museum, London.

COLOR PLATE I: Ch'êng Hua saucer with Three Friends—plum, bamboo and pine trees—growing near rock. Freer Gallery of Art, Washington, D.C.

plates were used to hold condiments such as candied violets and mints and were arranged on the cloth-covered rugs before the main course was presented.

This fine porcelain is only now beginning to be appreciated in the West. It was not one of the traditionally sought-after wares among Chinese collectors, perhaps because of the shadow cast upon it as a manufacture of the unhappy period of Mongol occupation. But its esthetic qualities bear comparison to the lauded early-fifteenth-century wares, which are the touchstone of Blue and White connoisseurship.

Yung Lo (1403–1424) and Hsüan Te (1426–1435)

From the time Blue and White was first collected in China, the wares of the early fifteenth century were the most prized. But appreciation in the West did not develop until recently. Now climbing prices at international auctions show how rapidly we are overcoming our former lack of insight. Here is the perfect Blue and White: full of forthright vitality, as balanced and rhythmic as a Baroque concerto, responsive to the fingertips, ripe and filling to the palm.

Genuine fifteenth-century pieces with the reign mark of Yung Lo are unknown, though the mark was used on wares of the Chêng Tê and T'ien Ch'i periods. But Hsüan Te reign marks are common, in fact so common that it seems unlikely that they all could have been made in the brief nine years of the reign. It has been suggested, and the idea seems credible, that the mark remained in currency until 1465, throughout the chaotic reigns of Chêng T'ung, Ching T'ai and T'ien Shun. The voluminous collections in the Middle East contain many examples of early-fifteenth-century wares, all of fairly high quality, but lacking marks. The bases of most of these and wares like them, apparently made for a moderately well-to-do domestic market and for export, are unglazed and are burned an apricot color. Some have drill marks, described by rows of holes, which identify the Persian or Turkish collections to which they once belonged.

The Hsüan Te mark was imitated in the late Ming reigns and throughout the Ch'ing dynasty, but a genuine specimen is not hard to recognize. The first

Early 15th century pilgrim flask with dragon amid lotus scrolls, key fret at lip. Courtesy Christie, Manson, and Woods, London.

character, *ta,* shows a strong, elongated diagonal dash to the lower right; and the third character, Hsüan, is usually contracted on its left side like an accordion. The mark may appear in two columns of three characters each within a double circle (the standard arrangement), or strung out horizontally, reading from right to left. The usual mark reads "great Ming Hsüan Te era made," arranged:

Te	ta		Te	great
nien	Ming		era	Ming
chih	Hsüan		made	Hsüan

Hsüan Te mark on white *lien tz'u* with *an hua* petal pattern. Courtesy Christie, Manson, and Woods, London.

The blue is a dark sapphire, full of flecks of pigment that give the "heaped-and-piled" effect. Though porcelains painted with the same batch of cobalt and fired side by side may show extremely different tones of blue because of the flow of smoke and other atmospheric conditions within the kiln, there are hues, such misfirings aside, that are characteristic of certain periods. A misfired piece is pale and silvery-grayish and gives little indication of the true color of the cobalt.

The glaze of Hsüan Te is often bluish or greenish, and is full of fine bubbles, but not so much so as to obscure the drawing beneath. On the surface the membrane of the bubbles has been broken, leaving the tiny pits that give good Blue and White its pleasing tactile qualities. The paste itself is very smooth and compact, and perfectly white.

The large, heavy serving utensils encountered among fourteenth-century wares continued to be made for the domestic and export markets, but a more refined ware has also survived; and a new repertoire of designs is evident in these. The painting is far better considered, the potting more precise, than in any of the earlier manufactures. A wide, conical bowl, called *ya shou pei* ("press hand cup"), and a hemispheric bowl that extends slightly to a point at the bottom, known as *lien tz'u* (lotus-pod bowl), were adapted from white wares. Flat-sided "moon flasks" (*yueh p'ing*) and discoidal pilgrim bottles with onion-shaped mouths (*pien hu*), made their appearance, as did a teapot-like wine ewer and the "monk's cap" jug.

The earliest of the traditional Imperial table services seem to date from the Hsüan Te period, and some of the patterns continued to be made until the end of the nineteenth century. Borders were restricted to a simple blue ring, but central motifs include dragons passant, ascending or descending, or amid clouds, flames or waterweeds; pairs of dragons disputing over pearls[6]; phoenixes; Three Friends (pine, bamboo and *Prunus* trees sprouting from behind a cactus-shaped rock);[7] sprays of carnations, peonies or five-petaled star-shaped flowers; bouquets of aquatic plants, and floral scrolls. Unlike the

[6] The dragon is a beneficent god of the skies, a rain god; he is also symbolic of the emperor. The phoenix is symbolic of the empress. The flaming pearl represents wisdom, in particular the wisdom of the balance of nature (*tao*).

[7] Symbolic of Buddha, Confucius, and Lao-tzu, and also of the three gentlemanly virtues, fortitude, integrity and optimism.

export wares, these are all thinly potted and have glazed bases. Also of fine quality but of heavier construction are stem cups, vases, leys jars (*cha tou*), *mei p'ing,* alms bowls, covered spherical bowls on stems and flowerpots.

The outline-and-wash technique was understood in the early Ming reigns, but there are few examples of it. Preferred was a brush stroke heavily laden with color, with details—such as dragon scales and the margins of flower petals—left white. The white gives a pleasing, highlighted effect. On the sturdy domestic and export wares, patterns in multiple bands continued to be popular, but the style of drawing became less free. The thumbprint look is gone from the wave border; the swells appear as neatly combed hillocks instead. The central motifs of the rock garden, and the clusters of fruit, all presented helter-skelter in the earlier ware, feel the pull of gravity and arrange

ABOVE: Early 15th century *lien tz'u* with petal pattern, key fret and wave pattern. Freer Gallery of Art, Washington, D.C.

OPPOSITE: Early 15th century *mei p'ing* of country manufacture with the cloud-hung Taoist paradise. Courtesy William H. Wolff, Inc., New York.

themselves with a definite top and bottom in the design. Decorations in white on a blue-washed ground are rare, but white dragons, with details incised in the paste against a background of waves, were introduced.

Rough wares made in the provinces, and in some commercial factories of Ch'ing-tê Chên, developed a sketchy style of decoration, which persisted throughout the Ming era, reaching a highpoint of skill and expressiveness at the end of the dynasty. Most abundant of the rough early-fifteenth-century pieces are jars and *mei p'ing* with scenes of figures in cloud-hung landscapes, representing the Taoist paradise. This early peasant ware has wide bands of border decorations on the shoulders and feet. Shoulder bands are usually of lotus scrolls, false gadroons, waves or brocade patterns broken by cartouches. The lower bands show stiff leaves, false gadroons or the wave-and-rock pattern known as the Taoist Isles of the Blest. (On pieces made in the late fifteenth and the sixteenth century, the Taoist paradise motif appears on a wide variety of shapes. Buildings, partly obscured by clouds, play a major part in the design, and the style of drawing shows the influence of woodblock book illustrations.) The white ground and the blue pigment of the earlier pieces are both distinctly grayish; and the glaze often fails to cover the body evenly, leaving jagged bare patches near the base. Later pieces have a clearer glaze that covers the body well, a whiter paste and a brighter blue.

Ch'êng Hua (1465–1487)

Genuine porcelains of this period are extremely rare; only some thirty pieces bearing the Ch'êng Hua mark are known. But imitations made in the eighteenth century, complete with Ch'êng Hua mark, are frequently encountered; and many pieces of the Chia Ching and Wan Li periods, though not in Ch'êng Hua style, bear the mark. Distinguishing genuine Ch'êng Hua from the excellent K'ang Hsi and Yung Chêng copies is one of the most trying problems in porcelain connoisseurship. But copies of the Ch'êng Hua reign mark made in the K'ang Hsi period usually display very small, precise characters strung out in two long vertical columns within a double circle. Marks of the Ch'êng Hua period have large, chunky characters that thoroughly fill the double circle[8] and seem almost cramped. However, all the genuine Ch'êng Hua pieces which are not of Imperial quality, and many which are, bear no marks at all.

The footring of fine Ch'êng Hua porcelains is deep and wedge-shaped in cross section, the inner wall being vertical and the outer wall slanting inward to form a rounded point at the edge. Where the biscuit is exposed on the footrim, the paste shows creamy smooth, more dense and unctuous than that of the K'ang Hsi and Yung Chêng copies. The glaze of genuine pieces is

[8] Ch'êng Hua marks may also be written within a double square or, as on the base of stem cups, in a horizontal line.

lustrous, perfectly even and dazzling, but not harsh in its brightness.

The potting of good Ch'êng Hua pieces and their imitations is "eggshell" thin. Shapes, on the basis of currently accepted examples, are limited, however, for most are of the Imperial table service sort. Little of the sturdy export ware or rougher provincial ware has been definitely identified as belonging to the period. A group of bowls with gracefully curving sides and slightly everted rims, about six inches in diameter, is known among dealers as palace bowls, though, for quibblers, there is no certain proof that they were ever used in the palace. A similar group of bowls is about eight inches in diameter. There are dishes seven inches to eight inches in diameter, stem cups and wine cups.

Imported cobalt ceased to be available in the Ch'êng Hua period, so the native pigment, refined as well as possible, had to be used. Chinese cobalt has traces of manganese in it that give the blue a slight violet tint. (A violet hue is also typical of K'ang Hsi wares and is a contributing factor in the difficulty of distinguishing between imitations and genuine pieces.) Careful refining of the cobalt removed almost all the little chunks of unground color which had given the "heaped-and-piled" effect. The smooth pigment permitted extensive use of an outline-and-wash technique. Decoration was drawn in a deep tone and filled in with diluted washes, the brush strokes of which show some overlapping. Highlights, especially the edges of petals, were left white; dark accents were carefully applied in concentrated color or several layers of wash. Late-fifteenth-century potters were still exploring the effects of graded washes, and some Ch'êng Hua pieces are distinctly streaky. K'ang Hsi potters, on the other hand, were expert at subtle and dramatic gradations. Their work may be recognized by a certain overmastery. "Boneless" (wash without outline) painting appears on some Ch'êng Hua pieces and their K'ang Hsi copies.

There is a variety of central motifs, but borders are usually restricted to a simple blue ring. Floral scrolls, restrained and serene, show surprising variations that break their symmetry. The Three Friends continued to be popular; so too did the spray of carnation, peony or five-petaled flowers. Stereotyped Buddhist and even Hindu emblems are the principal decorations on some pieces of moderate quality, though they are known only on rough wares prior to Ch'êng Hua. Taoist symbols and paradisiacal landscapes are also found. Fruiting vines, birds perched in trees and Fu dogs at play enjoyed a vogue; but formal dragons and phoenixes seem to have been out of fashion, and the few pieces that show them are not of the first quality. However, a strange dragon

Interior of Ch'êng Hua palace bowl showing floral scroll.
Freer Gallery of Art, Washington, D.C.

is associated with the period, though at least one is known with a Hsüan Te mark. This creature has an elephant's trunk, a floral scroll issues from its mouth, wings sprout from its shoulders, and instead of a belly and hind legs, its body abruptly terminates in leafy scrollwork.

Porcelains of coarse quality of this period are very difficult to identify, for there are no known pieces with reign marks or cyclical date marks to use as standards. Nevertheless, such wares must have been made. There are some pieces that, on grounds of their design and materials, must be placed between Hsüan Te and Chêng Tê. But it is best at present to refer to these simply as "late fifteenth century." There is considerable variety in their shapes. Many are familiar as slightly modified versions of Hsüan Te types. They will be dealt with in the following reign group.

However, there are a few less refined wares that are probably Ch'êng Hua. Among these are some rather heavily potted bowls ten to eleven inches in

Late 15th century bowl with figures in a landscape (possibly Ch'êng Hua). Freer Gallery of Art, Washington, D.C.

diameter, with straight rims. Fine, simply drawn decorations with carefully filled in washes adorn them. The drawings tend toward a feeling of spaciousness, for the elements of the design are a bit small for the areas they occupy. Figures in landscapes, aquatic scenes and duck ponds are favored. *An hua* ("secret decoration"), which is linear drawing incised in the porcelain body beneath the glaze, is known on this ware.

A decadent form of the lotus scroll, typical of Hung Chih, is first seen on rough Ch'êng Hua wares, and is the forerunner of the debased scroll that appears on sixteenth-century Blue and White. The "pendant-beads" detail, abundantly used on mid-sixteenth-century wares, also seems to have been introduced at this time.

Fine Ch'êng Hua is the rarest of intensely sought-after Blue and White. There are few pieces in American museums, though British museums seem to be somewhat better provided. Genuine pieces are all but unknown in the

LEFT: 16th century pear bottle with lotus scrolls, and borders of stiff leaves, key fret, *ju-i* scrolls and petals. The Metropolitan Museum of Art, New York, Gift of Paul E. Manheim, 1967.
RIGHT: Chêng Tê vase with Muhammadan scroll *(hui hui wen)*. Victoria and Albert Museum, London.

market. K'ang Hsi imitations, however, are extremely fine and worthy of appreciation in their own right.

Hung Chih (1488–1505)

As in the case of Ch'êng Hua, there are few known pieces of this reign that bear the reign mark. But Hung Chih was not a reign especially hailed for its porcelains, so the mark has not been copied. However, marked Hung Chih is of admirable quality, delicately potted and often "eggshell" thin. Fine plates and bowls predominate, as in the preceding reign. The footring is deep and slopes inward; and the base characteristically shows a slight convexity beneath.

The painting of Hung Chih is comparable to the not quite first-rate Ch'êng Hua pieces decorated with dragons.

Dragon motifs are seen on most Hung Chih pieces, the dragon appearing amid clouds, water weeds or lotus scrolls. But there are also porcelains decorated with inscriptions in Sanskrit, clouds or scenes of children at play (a motif called *wa wa*, after the onomatopoetic Chinese word for "children"). The Imperial tablewares decorated with floral sprays continued to be made during this period, and remained popular until the Chia Ching reign. The backgrounds of many of these pieces have been filled in with yellow enamel. The Sanskrit wares show characters more closely packed than on some similar porcelains thought to be Ch'êng Hua. The wave pattern was still in use in the Hung Chih period but had become debased; it appears either as a border or as a background, sketchily drawn in.

The principal motifs are those of Hsüan Te tablewares. But there is none of the "heaped-and-piled" effect in the Hung Chih; for the finely ground native cobalt was in use, and the blue is often grayish or pale, although it may appear quite bright when it is dense and near the surface. The outline-and-wash technique was favored, but the light of genius peculiar to Ch'êng Hua was lacking. The glaze is rich and smooth, with notable "dimpling" on the base. The Hung Chih mark is small, neat and well placed. Late pieces have large marks, apparently drawn by the same hand as Chêng Tê.

There is an assortment of late-fifteenth-century wares of lesser quality. These are sturdily built, in many cases intended for export. Persian shapes are seen in the ewers, *kendis* (rosewater sprinklers, later adapted as hookah bases), pilgrim flasks, vases, covered jars, small wine pots, basins and plates. Floral scrolls in the outline-and-wash technique decorate most pieces. The wash is flat and unhighlighted. Here are early examples of the decadent sixteenth-century lotus scroll, with its overcrowded design, uninspired placement of leaves and cramped style of drawing. A few specimens show cartouches, used as "cloud collars" or fitted together in radiating, snowflakelike patterns, filled with curlicues, flowers or birds. False gadroons, key fret, *ju-i* scrolls[9] and stiff leaf borders were used abundantly, beginning a renewed round of loading porcelains with row upon row of unrelated formal decorations.

[9] The *ju-i* is the sacred mushroom; its name is a homonym for "may everything be as you wish."

Painting is very like that of sixteenth-century wares, though often more roughly executed. It is in a grayish or blackish color, less intense than the Persian blue that came back into use in the Chia Ching period. Shapes recall Hsüan Te, but with odd proportions and some additions in questionable taste. The discoidal pilgrim flasks with onion mouths have a round, cuplike depression in the center of each flat side; ewers are broader and heavier in their silhouettes. Generally the porcelains are crude in potting and painting. It is from these, and not from the fine Hsüan Te and Ch'êng Hua tablewares that the styles of mass-produced porcelains of Chia Ching and Wan Li developed.

Chêng Tê (1506–1521)

The porcelains of this reign are transitional between the fine, delicate tablewares of Ch'êng Hua and the sturdy manufactures of the later sixteenth century. Middle Eastern influence prevails in most of the better pieces. Many bear inscriptions in Arabic or Persian—quotations from the Koran, aphorisms, or labels. The formal scrollwork that fills the corners and borders of these is not the familiar lotus, but a more abstract pattern called Muhammadan scroll (*hui hui wen*). This is drawn with an even, wide-spaced double line, and carefully filled in with ungraded wash. Some entirely abstract patterns are seen, such as 3-shaped scrolls. A motif suggesting a sprig of three cherries appears on some borders, and seems unique to Chêng Tê. The blue is still the soft-toned grayish native color, although where it is thick it may appear brilliant sapphire. The footrings of some large plates of this period slant sharply inward, echoing the angle of the sides of the vessels.

Muhammadans are reputed to have enjoyed considerable influence in the court of Chêng Tê, and many of the excellent porcelains in Middle Eastern taste may have been made for their use. Others, no doubt, were intended for the export market. In any case, a new assortment of shapes appears among the fine wares in *hui hui wen* style—square and cylindrical boxes, brush rests of stylized "mountain" or dragon form, table screens, hat stands, ink palettes and candlesticks. Dishes and bowls of equal quality are rare, though many of rough workmanship with Arabic or Persian inscriptions have been found. The Chêng Tê mark frequently appears on the good-quality Muhammadan wares, written in six characters within a double circle or square, or strung out horizontally within a double rectangle. The characters are large and fill the space well without appearing cramped.

Another group of porcelains belonging to the Chêng Tê period shows decorations of dragons amid busy floral scrolls. This style is shared by a two-color enameled porcelain on which the drawing is engraved in the paste and covered over with a translucent green enamel, while the background is filled in with yellow enamel. The shapes of the Blue and White examples, like the enameled ware, are limited to plates, bowls and basins, ewers, stem cups and *cha tou*. The debased floral scroll of the late sixteenth century is used in this design. There is a striking difference between this overcrowded, rather primitively drawn scroll, with its circular buds and tight little triangular petals, and the Muhammadan scroll, with its thick fronds and distended petals. The traditional lotus scroll, without dragons, appears on many vases of the period, with bands of formal decoration—stiff leaves, key fret, *j-ui* head scrolls and classical *ju-i* scrolls, and elements showing Muhammadan influence.

A thick, unctuous glaze, finely pitted and oily to the touch, is typical of Chêng Tê. On many pieces the blue pigment has run into the deep glaze with a blurred effect on the design; suspended bubbles may also give a hazy appearance. The cobalt is brilliant where it is concentrated and rises to the surface. The paste is fine and creamy; but potting is heavy. The Chêng Tê mark on the dragon scroll pieces is written in only four characters, and on other wares the Hsüan Te mark is imitated for the first time, for commendatory purposes.

Chêng Tê porcelains of the Imperial tableware sort are often difficult to distinguish from those of the late fifteenth century. But the stock designs of dragons, phoenixes, clouds and lotus scrolls suffer from stiffness and lack of spirit when compared with earlier pieces. The designs begin to show the unhappy indications of overfamiliarity; but they are beautifully painted, with even outlines and smooth washes. Their geometric precision suggests both the delicacy of Ch'êng Hua and the abstractness of *hui hui wen*.

Some small, rough jars are familiar manufactures of this and the following reign. These are crudely made, with stock designs of *wa wa*, phoenixes, lotus scrolls, dragons and Buddhist emblems, accompanied by borders of stiff leaves, false gadroons, key fret, and so forth. The jars are round, rectangular, or polygonal in cross section. The blue color is the native pigment and the paste is the compact Ma Ts'ang variety in the Chêng Tê specimens. Those of Chia Ching show the brighter imported cobalt and a grainier paste.

BELOW: Chêng Tê bowl with dragon amid lotus scrolls and *ju-i* head border at foot. The Metropolitan Museum of Art, New York, Fletcher Fund, 1925.

OPPOSITE: Chia Ching square jar of coarse manufacture with dragon amid floral scrolls. Museum of Fine Arts, Boston, John Gardner Coolidge Collection.

Chia Ching (1522–1566)

Wares of this period are not so finely made as those of the fifteenth century, for quantity rather than quality was stressed. But if the potting and painting are not the best, the vibrant tone of blue goes far to make up the loss; and the speedy deftness of design of many pieces is truly delightful. For these reasons, and because of their relative availability, Chia Ching Blue and White enjoys considerable popularity among collectors.

Several styles were shared by the Chia Ching, Lung Ch'ing, and Wan Li periods, and are usually classified simply as late sixteenth century. A strong influence of Taoism prevails in all. But the Muhammadan scroll is nowhere to be found. Favorite Taoist motifs include a peach tree twisted into a *shou* or other auspicious character, the eight trigrams of the *I-ching*,[10] deer, cranes, aquatic scenes, the Three Friends, Fu dogs and *wa wa*. Dragons and phoenixes are the most prevalent subjects, but they are stiff and stereotyped. The neck of the phoenix is reduced to an impossible foliate scroll, and the dragon takes on a look more surprised and comical than furious. Formal patterns of false gadroons, key fret, stiff leaves, and *ju-i* heads appear in abundance; a new design of widely spaced forget-me-nots enhances a few pieces; and some naturalistically draped flowering vines are particularly pleasing.

The commercial ware commonly decorated with Taoist paradisiacal land-scapes became more refined in this reign. As the tradition-bound Imperial por-celain declined in quality, the commercial wares improved. Novels illustrated with woodblock prints were popular at this time, and the private potteries, unrestricted by demands for traditional decoration, could experiment with styles of drawing adapted from the books. Landscapes took on the conventions of the block print, with shrubbery interpreted in spiky little knots of strokes, and hills and waves articulated with rows of combed lines beneath a blue wash. Subjects are whimsical and free in feeling, suggesting that pattern books were not strictly adhered to, and a single painter may have done each complete design. A growing trend toward individualism may be traced from these wares through the Transitional porcelains to K'ang Hsi.

Many new shapes came into fashion in the Chia Ching period, and there were some new interpretations of shapes borrowed from the fourteenth cen-tury. Dishes with foliate rims and fluted cavettos, pear-shaped bottles, vases with tall necks adorned with handles hung with rings, and *kuan* jars enjoyed a renewed popularity. Square dishes with gently sloping sides; double-gourd vases with upper and lower bulbs of almost equal size; round cushion-shaped,

---

10. The *I-ching* is an ancient mystical book of divination that employs the following fig-ures, adapted from Shang scapulamancy. The Shang prophecied by means of the markings on tortoise shells.

square, and oblong boxes and boxes with fluted corners, were introduced. The amount of tablewares seems small in proportion to the ornamental shapes in the later Ming reigns; but bowls of the Chia Ching period are distinct from all others, for they have convex, mounded centers. The Imperial tablewares with the floral spray motif ceased to be made.

Chia Ching–Wan Li vase with ear handles (often hung with loops), painted with draped peonies; peach sprays and cranes amid clouds on neck. Courtesy Frank Caro, New York.

The first wares expressly for the European market were made in this reign. These are rough pear-shaped bottles with bands painted around the shoulders enclosing inscriptions which seem to be Portuguese, albeit much misspelled. The earliest-known piece is dated 1541.

Imported cobalt was available in the reign of Chia Ching for the first time since Ch'êng Hua. Methods of careful refining that had been devised for the native cobalt were applied to the foreign pigment, and there is no evidence of the chips of blue that had caused the "heaped-and-piled" effect. The blue was used in dark, intense washes over an only slightly darker drawing; the result is nearly that of silhouette. Lighter washes were sometimes used, but rarely was an area of wash graded.

The paste of Chia Ching wares is not so smooth and compact as that of earlier reigns, for the mines at Ma Ts'ang, from which the finest kaolin was obtained, were depleted. The biscuit therefore appears neither so creamy to the touch nor so white. A grayish tinge is usually seen. The glaze is glossy, with a close, shallow pitting, and has an oily texture, much like that of Chêng Tê. A blurred effect occurs in the drawing when the glaze is thick, but it is rarely as apparent as on pieces of the previous reign.

The Chia Ching mark, written in six characters, appears either within a double circle or simply drawn on the base in circular order, to be read clockwise, with no enclosing double circle or double square. Ch'êng Hua and Hsüan Te marks were often used for commendatory purposes in this and later reigns; but they were applied with no intention to deceive, for the pieces on which they appear do not even imitate the earlier styles. Even when, in the Ch'ing dynasty, Ming marks appear on extremely deceptive copies, there is none of the onus of forgery involved. Imitations were regarded as the highest achievements of skill (this is true in potting, as in Chinese painting) and reflected great honor on the potters. It must be remembered that China was a country of ancestor worship, untouched by the Western cult of progress.

Lung Ch'ing (1567–1572)

The known porcelains of Lung Ch'ing are hardly distinguishable in style from those of the surrounding reigns of Chia Ching and Wan Li. The blue is the imported pigment, applied heavily to produce an intense color. As with

Chia Ching, the washes are often so dark as to nearly obscure the drawing, resulting in a silhouette effect. The quality of the drawing is usually poorer than Chia Ching, and somewhat sketchy. Most pieces are of private manufacture, for the Imperial factory was closed during much of the reign. A few fine boxes of novel shape, bowls, plates, cups and teapots with handles arching above their lids are known.

According to the *T'ao Shuo,* Lung Ch'ing had porcelains decorated with erotic subjects, but none of these has appeared in modern collections.

Wan Li bowl with dragon amid clouds pursuing "flaming pearl." Courtesy Christie, Manson, and Woods, London.

Wan Li (1573–1619)

Blue and White porcelains of the last significant reign of the Ming dynasty are stylistically much like those of Chia Ching. The decoration of Imperial wares was limited to traditional motifs, the spirit of which had long since begun to fade. The phoenixes, dragons and floral scrolls all bespeak method rather than imagination. The popular *wa wa,* scenes of interiors with figures and sages in landscapes have a crowded feeling, further heightened by the use of multiple brocade borders. Cranes, deer, peach trees and aquatic scenes— all subjects with Taoist associations—remained the staples of the decorator's repertoire, but are most often seen on pieces of middling quality.

The whimsical, sketchy style introduced on the lower grade of commercial wares of Chia Ching is evident on more pieces and is seen in a wider variety of subjects, capturing for all of them a warmth and humor inaccessible to the mechanically drawn and filled-in Imperial porcelains. This Blue and White presents another link in the developing humanized technique of the commercial porcelain painter. Wan Li examples include the last uses of the combed line effect superimposed on washes, and also show a linear, "penciled" style of drawing in which a line of even width is used and washes are omitted. A similarly sketchy style is also used with light washes; this developed into a style favored in the T'ien Ch'i reign.

The blue color, mostly the native product, is pale and grayish; rarely, even on Imperial products, does it reach the intensity of the Chia Ching pigment. The porcelain body is also slightly grayish and coarse. Many pieces are of an earthy, friable material, from which the glaze is likely to flake. This is a defect associated with *kraakporselein,* but there is really very little difference between the export and the domestic, low-grade commercial wares of Wan Li.

Decorative and functional porcelains other than tablewares predominate in the middle- and fine-quality ranges of Wan Li Blue and White. The potting of these is heavy, and lacks precision. Shapes are ornate. Square, cushion-shaped and fluted-cornered boxes were still very much in vogue, as were vases, ewers, teapots, incense burners, brush handles, pricket candlesticks, beakers, pen rests in the shape of dragons, covered jars, jars of monumental proportions, little rouge boxes and *kendis* (not only of the usual hookah shape, but also shaped like elephants or frogs). Formal motifs decorate most of these.

The Wan Li mark appears in six characters within a double circle, or circularly written without an enclosing double circle or square. All the reign marks of the fifteenth century were used with equanimity by Wan Li potters. The contracted footring, tapering inward toward the edge, continued to be formed on cups and bowls, as it had been in the Chia Ching period. Chatter marks, radiating gouges made when the foot was carelessly formed and not smoothed over, appear on the bases of some pieces.

Some Wan Li and Transitional Blue and White was influenced by a white ware that reached its perfection in the Wan Li period. This was the *ling lung* ("devil's work"), plain white porcelain with elaborate brocade patterns pierced through the sides. Low-relief cartouches of tiny landscapes with figures in full relief were added for further ornament. Occasionally painting in under-glaze blue was used in place of the expensive pierced work.

Designs reserved in white against a blue-washed ground reappear among Chia Ching and Wan Li porcelains, revived for the first time since Hsüan Te. Details were either carved in the body beneath the glaze in *an hua* fashion, or drawn in blue.

A group of rough jars with lobed sides, a grayish paste and freely executed designs (usually fruit, birds and growing bushes or floral scrolls) belong to this and the Chia Ching period. Some coarse tablewares decorated with in-scriptions in Sanskrit are also of late Ming manufacture and came from factories on the southeast coast. A large character appears in the center, with rows of repeated characters on the sides. These are rougher than the similar early-fifteenth-century examples; the body material is impure and grayish, the pigment grayish violet. A number of porcelains of very rough construc-tion and naïve decoration were made at various times at the peasant kilns on the southern coast, but these will be dealt with below, under the heading "Provincial Ming Export Wares."

T'ien Ch'i (1621–1627) and Ch'ung Chêng (1628–1643)

There are very few wares bearing the marks of either of these reigns; but those that are known are of rough quality, more akin to the cheapest porcelains of commercial manufacture than to Imperial products. Bushell[11] records a

[11] *Oriental Ceramic Art,* p. 257.

ABOVE: Late 16th century jar of rough manufacture with lobed sides, painted with birds and sprouting peonies. Courtesy The Asian Gallery, New York.

BELOW: T'ien Ch'i tub-shaped incense burner with flowers in "boneless" style. The British Museum, London.

T'ien Ch'i export plate in cartoon style for Japanese market *(ko-sometsuke)*. Victoria and Albert Museum, London.

Wan Li covered bowl with biscuit figures in relief in *ling lung* style. Background painted with landscapes. The Metropolitan Museum of Art, New York.

group of water jars simply marked "T'ien" ("Heaven"), painted in a blue comparable to good examples of Wan Li; but other than these, T'ien Ch'i is far below the standards of earlier reigns. The drawing is sketchy; the pigment is grayish or violet; the potting is rough; and the paste is gray. Bases show chatter marks, and sometimes accretions of sand.

A "boneless" style of painting is seen on a cylindrical incense burner with the T'ien Ch'i mark. The petals of the flowers are simply soft-toned circular washes of color; stems, tendrils and leaves are in dark, washy strokes. Fine line drawing is used for detail rather than outline.

A more common but unmarked variety of Blue and White of the T'ien Ch'i period shows the lively, sketchy, cartoonlike style of drawing inherited from the Wan Li commercial potters. Human figures are the favored subject matter, and they are frequently presented in unconventional scenes. A plate in the Victoria and Albert Museum depicts a number of naked people under a tree, apparently engaged in a game of blindman's buff. These drawings are simple and linear, with washes used as accents or to fill in areas, such as clumps of leaves or fishermen's nets. Plates are most common. Though not finely made, in decoration these are among the most delightful of porcelains. They have always been held in high regard in Japan, and were principally made for export to that country.

Few porcelains are known to bear the mark of Ch'ung Chêng. A plate reproduced in Garner's *Oriental Blue and White* shows a dragon affrontée in a linear drawing without wash. The dragon is dignified but has a strong sense of immediacy. But the pieces identifiably of Ch'ung Chêng are hardly sufficient in number to make any statements about the style of the ware in general.

It seems most likely that the Imperial factory was closed during the reigns of T'ien Ch'i and Ch'ung Chêng. If any porcelain was made for palace use, it was probably commissioned from the commercial potteries of Ch'ing-tê Chên. Such an occurrence would account for the total disappearance of porcelains of Imperial quality and the subsequent introduction of the sophisticated but untraditional Transitional wares among the commercial manufactures. These seem to have been made by the former Imperial potters, working on their own, though no documents beyond the wares themselves have yet come to light to support such an assumption. While the sketchy wares for the Japanese market, known as *ko-sometsuke,* are thought to be specifically of the T'ien Ch'i period, the finer Transitional wares are considered to belong to the reigns of Ch'ung Chêng and the first Ch'ing, Shun Chih.

Kraakporselein (Wan Li and T'ien Ch'i European Export Ware)

The Dutch name *kraakporselein* seems worth perpetuating, not only for its historical associations but also as a convenient means for distinguishing the rough crockery exported in large quantities to the West at the end of the seventeenth century from the more elaborate wares of the same period. Coarse porcelains, intended for daily household use, no doubt, were made from the time underglaze painting became a familiar medium; but like all uncherished crockery, most examples must be assumed to have perished long ago. Only in those countries where porcelain itself was a rare and exotic substance can we expect to find specimens of the ware. Thus it is in Philippine burial grounds that early Ming Blue and White of the commonest quality is found, and in European and American museums and collections that late Ming poor man's Blue and White is seen.

The body material of the porcelain is dry and crisp in consistency. Because of the earthiness of the biscuit, the glaze does not adhere as closely as on finer wares, and some flaking may result, especially on sharp rims. The potting is thin. Cups, bowls and plates are often molded in fluted or petal patterns of raised panels. The white ground is grayish on most pieces; the blue is pale and lavender, grayish, or blackish when it is heavily applied. But some specimens show the sapphire blue more common on Transitional wares. Footrings are rough, chatter marks appear on bases, and bits of sand and grit lie embedded in the margin of the glaze. Most pieces bear no mark at all, but a scrawled plum branch is often seen on the reverse sides of plates and saucers.

A typical example of *kraakporselein* shows a decoration divided into panels, either simply painted or further accentuated by the molded body. A central panel fills the mirror of plates, bowls and cups, and smaller panels radiate from it. Favorite motifs for the center include dragons, a bird or an insect perched on a rock, rabbits or deer in a wood, mandarin ducks on a pond and kylins[12] standing on wave-spattered rocks. The radiating panels contain diaper patterns, pendant jewels or bows, alternated with "precious objects" or auspicious symbols, floral sprays or repetitions of the central motif.

Kraakporselein was particularly popular in Holland and northern Europe; examples of it figure in many Dutch paintings of still lifes and interiors. It was this ware that inspired the design of Delft. Japanese imitations of *kraakporselein* were purchased by the Dutch at Deshima, but never in such quantities as the Chinese product. The Japanese examples differ stylistically from the Chinese, particularly in the understanding of border panel motifs.

The Western love for *kraakporselein* resulted in the embellishment of many pieces with silver or silver-gilt mounts. Though these may obscure the porcelain itself, they serve to remind us of the reverence in which the ware was held; and they are usually quite handsome in their own right.

---

[12] Kylins are mythical beasts with hooves and leonine heads. They were believed to inhabit the Isles of the Blest, and to be so gentle as to take great care not to step on insects.

ABOVE: *Kraakporselein* plate with paneled decoration and central motif of a bird on a rock. Courtesy The Asian Gallery, New York.
BELOW: 17th century Japanese imitation of *kraakporselein* with central motif of an insect on a rock. Courtesy The Asian Gallery, New York.

Provincial Ming Export Wares

Several types of Blue and White porcelains originated in rural workshops during the Ming and Ch'ing dynasties. These were common crockeries intended for local use, but some pieces were exported to the Philippines, Indonesia and southeast Asia. Most of the factories with which we are concerned were located in the southern coastal provinces of Fukien, Chekiang and Kwangtung; this is because only their wares were exported and preserved. Though similar porcelains were made in the inland provinces, we shall deal only with the wares that are familiar outside of China.

Typically, this provincial export ware is very rough and heavily potted, with a distinctly gray or brownish body and a pale grayish or blackish pigment. Bowls, cups, plates and large and small jars predominate. Excavations in the Philippines date the wares found there from the Yüan dynasty to the

Provincial Ming export bowl with freely drawn "circle-and-dot" pattern. The British Museum, London.

reign of Chia Ching; but similar country Blue and White is still being made. Modern pieces, though decorated in the same styles, show a perfectly white body and a clear glaze.

One of the oldest wares still manufactured shows a free, scrawling decoration of circles, spirals and dots. Washes are used to draw broad lines, but there is no outline-and-wash. The complete abstractness of these designs is surprising and quite appealing. Most pieces are bowls, thinly potted and a bit asymmetric, with a knife-trimmed lip. The glaze of examples from the Philippines is often deteriorated because of burial, leaving the blackish-blue painting to stand out in sharp contrast against a brownish-yellowish-gray mat ground. These vessels, and others decorated with briskly dashed-off sunflowers, were highly prized by the Pacific island dwellers and were buried within the grave wrappings of their dead. Plates and jars were also used as grave gifts, and large jars were employed as coffins for infants.

A ware similar to the above, but more roughly made, with a badly pitted surface, a rounded lip and a wobblier shape, is thought to have come from the western province of Szechwan. The body of these is gray, and the glaze brownish. Painting is in a soft grayish or lavender blue. The motifs are not so abstract as those of the circle-and-dot ware, for landscapes, flowers and figures can be discerned.

A group of small jars with high shoulders and little, flaring necks is also found in the Philippines and Indonesia. These have a thick, bubbly glaze which is subject to crazing, and a dry, earthy body. The decoration is in an outline-and-wash technique; elements may even be outlined and reserved in white. The painting is divided into panels with formal border motifs. Taoist subjects such as deer and rabbits are favored. This ware seems to have been made at the end of the Ming dynasty and during the Transitional period.

A better-known variety of Ming export porcelain is that called Swatow, after its port of embarkation. Its place of manufacture is unknown. Two distinct types are recognized. One is freely and deftly painted in a style most readily described as "loaded brush," for the brush was so full of wet pigment that each stroke terminates with a dark drop of color. Designs are composed of broad strokes, with no attempt at outline and wash. The floral sprays, kylins, Fu dogs and phoenixes all have a pleasant country-kitchen look. Plates and large jars with loop handles on the shoulders are most common. The white ground is dirty-looking; the blue is grayish-black; the base is rough, messy and full of sand or gravel. The other Swatow ware is copiously decorated with brocade borders, cartouches and panels, with lush, almost undecipherable scenes of flora and fauna in the center panel. The white shows grayish blue, with painting in a soft lavender or grayish blue. *Kraakporselein* springs to mind, but Swatow is more elaborate.

Another provincial export ware of the Ming dynasty is recognized by a brush stroke so broad and washy as to suggest finger painting. Appropriately, the motifs are childlike and delightfully naïve. The glaze is of a low gloss, yellowish to cream color, and may be netted with close crazing. The blue is pale grayish or blackish. Again, it is the large jars with loop handles on the shoulders that are most often seen. These jars were constructed by the coil method, in which the clay is rolled between the potter's hands to form a long rope, then coiled layer upon layer to build the desired shape. This manner of

OPPOSITE: Ming Swatow jar with floral sprays, classic scroll and fanciful bird in the "loaded brush" style. The British Museum, London.
ABOVE: Ming Swatow plate with central motif of a bird on a bough; diapered border with cartouches. Courtesy The Asian Gallery, New York.

potting was abandoned by the mainstream of Chinese ceramic manufacture when the wheel came into common use, before 1500 B.C.

There are numerous other types of Blue and White country wares, for most peasant potteries had something to offer as Blue and White. Scholarship is slow to deal with wares that lack great antiquity, great expense or historical associations to recommend them. So until methodical excavations are made at old kiln sites, and the types of shards common to them recorded and published, we must appreciate these simple, unpretentious objects solely for what their appearance conveys.

BELOW: Chia Ching miniature teacup of commercial quality with fanciful landscape showing "combed" hills. 2⅞ in. diameter.
OPPOSITE, LEFT: K'ang Hsi club-shaped vase with landscape showing "blazed" rocks. Museum of Fine Arts, Boston, James Fund.
RIGHT: Transitional covered jar with landscape, and incised *an hua* decoration on shoulder. Courtesy Mr. and Mrs. Carroll L. Cartwright.
COLOR PLATE II: Chia Ching covered sweetmeats box with pheasant perched on a *mu t'an* (tree) peony, diaper border with cartouches (see Swatow version of pattern, page 65). Courtesy Mr. and Mrs. Carroll L. Cartwright.

Transitional Wares (1627–1683)

"Transitional" is a convenient, informal term used to designate a group of porcelains commercially manufactured at Ch'ing-tê Chên from the end of the T'ien Ch'i period until the appointment of Ts'ang-ying Hsüan as director of the Imperial factory in the reign of K'ang Hsi. Despite the intangibility of their origin, these porcelains have a unifying sense of style, workmanship and high quality of materials. Characteristically, the paste is bright white, smooth and compact; but small spots that the glaze has not covered (called "bare bones") may be burned black, and large unglazed areas, such as the bottoms of vases, show patchy burns in apricot color. The glaze is unctuous, suffused with fine bubbles, but clear, or slightly greenish or bluish in tint. The cobalt is a well-refined native variety, with a deep, rich violet tone. Superimposed dabbings of the brush create subtle gradations of color; and dramatic blendings from white to dark violet are seen, especially in the white blaze that runs down the side of rocks and mountains in landscapes.

Decorative conventions unique to Transitional wares are borders of tight little scrolls incised in the body beneath the glaze, elaborate tuliplike flowers in a style surprisingly suggestive of Pennsylvania Dutch, and towering cliffs interlaced with clouds. This last is applied as a means of adapting a book illustration to a vase surface when the opposite ends of the picture cannot otherwise be joined. Other popular motifs include plantain trees, naturalistic growing plants, waterfowl at the margins of ponds, landscapes with animals or figures, and figure subjects. Many of the landscapes and figures were borrowed from book illustrations.

Painting is of exceptional quality; plants are more botanically "true" than ever before, landscapes are more thorough and figures more animated. Formal borders continued to be used on some pieces, but most have no borders at all, showing an uncommon but welcome amount of white space.

Potting is heavy, and bases poorly finished; but many handsome and inventive shapes appear. Wide, beakerlike vases, cylindrical bottles with high shoulders and short, flaring necks, oval jars with cap covers, were all introduced. Austerity seems the key to the freshness of the new forms. Some shapes, such as tankards and salt cellars, were made to order for the European market. But for the most part the potters seem to have been left to their own discretion. Vases predominate. Most pieces are unmarked; but a few bear date marks, Ming reign marks, auspicious symbols or commendatory phrases.

Transitional porcelains are important for their intrinsic beauty, and for their historical significance as the culmination of the style of the Ming commercial potters and the bridge to the ceramics of K'ang Hsi. Much of the ware was exported to the West at the time of its manufacture, for European trade was at a peak of demand; and the domestic market was depressed because of the unsettled interregnum. For this reason Transitional porcelain is still available in sufficient quantity to be collected by the alert browser.

K'ang Hsi (1662–1722)

Although the Imperial porcelain factory was operative in the early years of the Ch'ing dynasty, it was not until 1683, when Ts'ang-ying Hsüan arrived as its director, that Ch'ing porcelain manufacture began in earnest. The following century was to see more innovations in decoration than had been attempted ever before. The two major palettes for overglaze enameling, the *famille verte* and the *famille rose,* were developed, and numerous monochrome and polychrome glazes were devised. Nevertheless, Blue and White held its popularity throughout the K'ang Hsi reign, coasting on the momentum of innovation built up in the Transitional period. Many new styles appeared, and a new clay was discovered.

Though the sources of the chief components—kaolin and petuntse for body and glaze, and cobalt for pigment—changed at various times, subtly affecting the appearance of the ware, Blue and White ideally remained a smooth-surfaced, hard white porcelain with a clear, even glaze. But the introduction of a new body material provided a variation on that ideal. The clay is called *hua shih.* Ceramics made of it are known as *chiang t'ai,* "paste-bodied." From a translation of the Chinese, the Western term for it, "soft paste," is derived; but this is confusing, for *chiang t'ai* is entirely unlike the "soft paste" of European manufacture. The chief ingredient of *hua shih* is pegmatite; there is no ground glass as there is in European "soft paste." *Hua shih* could be used either for the entire body of a vessel, or, in diluted form, as a slip to cover regular porcelain. *Chiang t'ai* wares are lighter in weight than porcelain, and opaque, with a creamy, yellowish or dead-white color. Usually the glaze shows a netting of brown crackle, or the surface undulates with little lumps, called

Ch'ien Lung *chiang t'ai* ("soft paste") rouge box with Hundred Antiques motif. Courtesy of The Brooklyn Museum.

"chicken skin." *Hua shih* has a soft, earthy quality, far less compact than good kaolin, yet it can be delicately modeled. Apparently the substance was very expensive, for vessels of it were costly at the time of manufacture. Vases and small articles for the scholar's table predominate. *Hua shih* provides a particularly receptive ground for fine line painting. Designs are very delicate. Landscapes in the styles of classical scroll painting are favored. Most pieces belong to the Yung Chêng and Ch'ien Lung periods, and even these are rare.

The traditional materials of Blue and White of the K'ang Hsi period are much the same as those of the Transitional and seem to have come from the same sources. The blue is rich and violet, and is painted in fine gradations. The white body is somewhat more refined and brilliant than on the Transitional wares, gently blending with the glaze to give a translucent, milky ground. The glaze is glossy and colorless.

K'ang Hsi marks, as mentioned above, are written in small characters that form two elongated vertical columns. Hsüan Te or Ch'êng Hua marks are common, especially on pieces imitating the classics of those periods. Often no mark at all appears, only an empty double ring. On a few late Imperial pieces the K'ang Hsi mark is written in three vertical rows of two characters each. Sym-

BELOW, LEFT: K'ang Hsi covered goblet painted in the "feathery flower" style. The Metropolitan Museum of Art, New York.

RIGHT: K'ang Hsi double-gourd vase painted with "tiger-lily" pattern; rudimentary sketch for band of "cracked ice" at lip. The Metropolitan Museum of Art, New York, Bequest of William Rhinelander Stewart, 1929.

OPPOSITE: K'ang Hsi saucer, cross-hatched silhouette decoration divided into radiating panels. The Metropolitan Museum of Art, New York.

bolic marks such as flowers, artemisia leaves and rabbits are also seen.

A great many decorative innovations belong to the K'ang Hsi period, but most of the more oddly stylized ones are specifically associated with wares of commercial quality. Among these are the so-called "tiger-lily pattern," a busy motif of feathery flowers, and a style in which the decorative elements are outlined in silhouette, then filled in with cross-hatching. Another new style presents white flowers and branches surrounded by a blue cloudlike wash to help them stand out against the otherwise plain white background. A very different white-on-blue-on-white style of the period was adapted from ancient bronzes. A *t'ao t'ieh* (ogre mask) or other device was painted on these in blue wash over the white ground; details of the mask were reserved in white.

White decoration reserved on a blue ground is seen on various wares, beginning in the fourteenth century, but on no porcelains is it more effective than on the famous "hawthorn jars." The pattern of these vessels, actually depicting plum blossoms, shows white branches festooned with white flowers against a "cracked-ice" ground. "Cracked ice" is achieved by dividing the ground into angular cells lightly drawn in blue, then filling the cells with graded washes to give a translucent, faceted effect. The intent is to suggest

thawing ice cracking on the surface of a stream. This motif has been imitated both in China and in Japan, but only the finest early examples attain a true "cracked ice"; copies show either lines too heavily drawn, with a broad, clumsy grading of washes, or washes applied in broad scallops, like finger painting, with no attempt at facets. The plum-branch-and-ice theme is associated with the New Year; for the plum tree is said to blossom at that time, providing the first sign of the coming spring. Hawthorn jars were used to hold New Year's presents; the jars themselves were returned to the giver after their contents had been removed. In the nineteenth century tea or ginger was packed in them. Formal, rather stiff floral scrolls are also reserved in white against blue on vases of the K'ang Hsi period and their imitations.

The landscape and figure styles of the Transitional period were developed during the K'ang Hsi reign. There is no crowding or stiffness in these; the

OPPOSITE: K'ang Hsi vase with white magnolias accentuated by "clouds" of blue wash. The Metropolitan Museum of Art, New York, The H.O. Havemeyer Collection. BELOW: K'ang Hsi hawthorn jar. Copyright The Frick Collection, New York.

K'ang Hsi plate with "cuckoo in the house" pattern, possibly of Dutch origin. The Metropolitan Museum of Art, New York.

openness, vitality and humor of the earlier ware are still to be seen. But dragons, phoenixes, kylins, Fu dogs and *wa wa* were popular too. The K'ang Hsi dragon has a bulbous, down-turned nose and is quite furious of mein. Among these wares, made for the reviving domestic market, there are a number of styles associated with the *famille verte* enamels; these include a design of blossoms and galloping horses strewn over spiral "waves," some historic and domestic scenes and floral subjects that recall the colored-ground *famille jaune* and *famille noire*.

An austere group comprising vases and eggshell-thin scholars' accessories with restrained decoration shows either tight, formal sunburst medallions with a border of triangles at the base, or *fa lung* (the familiar celestial dragon) or *chih lung* (a lizardlike archaic dragon seen mostly in jade carving). These porcelains are of the finest quality; they are of late manufacture and show the reign mark in three vertical rows of characters. There are more examples in underglaze red than blue.

K'ang Hsi shapes are lively and inventive. Cylindrical club-shaped vases,

K'ang Hsi plate showing the 1690 riots in Rotterdam, after a European engraving. Courtesy Mr. and Mrs. Carroll L. Cartwright.

fat egg-shaped jars with cap covers, square vases, trumpet-mouthed vases, are all frequently seen; and the first *garniture de cheminée,* (sets of three covered jars and two beakers) make their appearance. Generally K'ang Hsi forms suggest a dynamic upward motion. Though Yung Chêng and Ch'ien Lung wares employ much of the same repertoire of shapes, the former seem to have a downward weighting, while the latter, a perfectly centered swelling. Forms derived from ancient bronzes were imitated in Ch'ing vase shapes throughout the dynasty.

Much Blue and White was still made for export to the West. European ceramic, glass and metal shapes are recognizable among these. Monteiths, shell-shaped dishes, tankards, covered goblets and vases with wiggly handles copied from Venetian glass are seen. Patterns favored for the least expensive export tablewares include brocades, floral motifs, "Long Elizas" (a pattern nicknamed by the Dutch) and baskets of flowers (*hua lan,* symbolic of the Taoist genie Lan Ts'ai-ho, one of the Eight Immortals).

Some export tableware was decorated with subjects derived from European engravings. These are often delightfully comical in their renderings of scenes bizarre to the decorator but familiar to Westerners. Subjects from the Bible and Greek mythology and even a view of the 1690 riots in Rotterdam are encountered. Most interesting of the religious illustrations is a group intended for the Japanese Christian market. Western style is not attempted; the Crucifixion is presented in Japanese taste with Oriental figures.

K'ang Hsi Blue and White was in demand, at incredibly high prices, in Europe and America at the beginning of this century. This was partly due to the influence of James McNeill Whistler, who was an ardent early collector. Popularity coincided with a time of abundant export, so the ware is not difficult to find. With museums filled to surfeit and collectorly attention centered on fifteenth- and sixteenth-century porcelains, K'ang Hsi is now neglected; though the inveterate antique hunter probably never will find a piece of Hsüan Te, or even Chêng Tê, in a dusty corner of an attic or shop, it is quite likely he may find some excellent pieces of K'ang Hsi. Here is a perfect ware for a beginning collector. The innate quality of this Blue and White is beyond question, for K'ang Hsi is a period truly marked by inspiration in porcelain manufacture. It will, no doubt, eventually return to favor.

Yung Chêng (1723–1735)

Porcelains of the Yung Chêng period are noted for their delicacy and precise finish. This is no less true of Blue and White than of the *famille rose,* for which the reign is especially famous. But by the eighteenth century, the impetus for invention had been diverted from underglaze painting to the newer mediums of enameling and monochrome and polychrome glazes. Blue and White dominated Ming manufacture, but in the later Ch'ing it would only echo its former successes. Copies of Hsüan Te, Ch'êng Hua and Chia Ching were produced for the court, in keeping with the ultraconservative tastes of the Manchu dynasty.

Chia Ching imitations are in a rich lavender blue. The designs—formal scrolls, *Shou* or other characters of well-wishing, dragons, phoenixes, cranes or other Taoist subjects—are always far more clean and precise than anything a Chia Ching potter would have conceived. As imitations they are too perfect;

Yung Chêng saucer in Chia Ching style, decorated with a character, peach boughs and *ju-i*. Courtesy The Asian Gallery, New York.

as an independent style, they are very pleasing.

Ch'êng Hua imitations are painted in a pale, silvery blue. Since Yung Chêng ware is precise, feminine and delicate, it is informed by an esthetic very similar to that of Ch'êng Hua; copies cannot be distinguished by too fine a finish. Fortunately, most Yung Chêng pieces are correctly marked, or so it seems.

The simulations of Hsüan Te are the least effective. In an attempt to imitate the "heaped-and-piled" look of fifteenth-century ware, Yung Chêng potters carefully painted speckles along the lines of their drawings. The regularity in shape and spacing of the dots immediately belies them. Floral scrolls or sprays of fruit or flowers are the chief subjects. Painting is cramped, the elements being too small for the space they occupy. To counteract the resulting empty space, more is crowded onto the porcelain surface. Nevertheless the style remained popular throughout the Ch'ien Lung period. Middle- to late-eighteenth-century examples are carefully painted, in a blackish blue, but the background has a chalky, dead look when compared to the silvery Yung Chêng white.

Ch'ien Lung basin with unusual composition of a dragon and a
fish amid combed waves. Museum of Fine Arts, Boston, John
Gardner Coolidge Collection.

Tablewares predominate in the Ch'êng Hua and Chia Ching styles. Ornamental objects were preferred for the Hsüan Te. Among the more freely
decorated commercial porcelains, shapes also hearken to early-fifteenth-century
types. Pilgrim bottles, both of the simple discoidal shape and of the discoidal
shape topped with an onion-shaped mouth are seen. Stem cups and conical
bowls adapted from the *ya shou pei* are not uncommon.

A number of decorative subjects borrowed from rare pieces of Hsüan Te
reentered the painter's repertoire at this time and remained standard for the
next century. Among these is a stiff rendition of the Eight Buddhist Emblems
of Happy Augury—paired fish, the flaming wheel of the Law, the endless
knot, the lotus, the canopy, the umbrella of state, the conch shell and the vase;
and the Eight Precious Objects—a pair of books, a coin, a painting, a round
jewel, an artemisia leaf, a lozenge symbol of victory, a right-angle jade musical
stone, and a pair of rhinoceros-horn cups. All are presented hovering above
the flowers of a formal lotus scroll. A style of heavy linear drawing became
popular for figure subjects, especially the Eight Immortals Crossing the Sea.

An innovation of the K'ang Hsi period that enjoyed a vogue in the Yung

Chêng and Ch'ien Lung reigns is a technique known as "scratched blue." The design was lightly incised in the paste; then the grooves were filled with blue, or sometimes apple-green pigment, and colorless glaze was applied over the entire vessel. The effect is of a barely visible fine line drawing with a corresponding indentation on the surface of the glaze.

Yung Chêng Blue and White shows a lustrous, silvery-white porcelain. The blue is slightly lavender, or blackish where it is applied thickly. The glaze is smooth and even but may be suffused with fine bubbles. Tiny pinholes in the glaze may appear as brownish-black burned specks in even the most highly finished of Chinese porcelains and Yung Chêng is no exception; these are not considered flaws.

Here again is a porcelain of quality which has not received the interest it deserves. But, unlike K'ang Hsi, it is far from a collector's haven, for Yung Chêng is rare. Two reasons account for this: first, the brevity of the reign; second, the greater interest in other decorative techniques at the time.

Ch'ien Lung (1736–1795)

This is the last period to be seriously considered by traditional connoisseurship; and it is not Blue and White, but monochromes and the *famille rose,* that are held most important. Ch'ien Lung Blue and White must, for the most part, be confessed to be unexciting; but the dullness of the ware is here and there relieved by pieces of startlingly beautiful design. Humor, highly imaginative composition and painstaking technique combine to redeem the few. The rest, relying on technique alone, are oppressive. Floral and landscape painting is more elaborate than ever before. The blaze on rocks has been replaced by laborious hatching, and all the various brush strokes of classical scroll painting are displayed.

Much Ch'ien Lung Blue and White imitates Ming, but with less success than in the previous reign. The painting is nearly equal, but materials declined in quality. Blue is blackish; white has a dead look; the glaze is glassy. The ware has less vibrancy and tactile deliciousness than its predecessors.

Favorite stock motifs include dragons, phoenixes, figures in gardens, close views of rock gardens (adapted from the *famille rose*), peaches with bats (a rhebus for Happiness and Longevity: *shou fu*). Export wares decorated

Chia Ch'ing plate with motif of the Eight Immortals Crossing the Sea. The Metropolitan Museum of Art, New York.

with subjects from European engravings again were popular. Biblical, classical and contemporary illustrations are all found. The quality of the drawing varies from quaintly Oriental to nearly perfectly "Western," but the least polished are usually the most delightful. In these we see Triumphs of Chinese Poseidons, and *wa wa* masquerading as cherubim. The discovery of black

Commercial quality Chia Ch'ing plate. Border shows attributes of the Eight Immortals; central motif of drunken man returning home aided by servants.

enamel renewed interest in the copying of engravings, and Blue and White served as an economical version of the more expensive enameled ware.

Two innovations date from the Ch'ien Lung reign. One is the occasional use of an overglaze enamel of a rich sapphire color, instead of underglaze painting. Wares of this sort are not, properly speaking, of the Blue and White family.

The other is a piercing technique, seen on wares called Rice Grain. The body of these vessels, usually bowls, is pierced with elliptical, rice-grain shaped holes arranged in lacy patterns. Unpierced areas are painted in blue. When the vessel was glazed, the glaze filled the holes, forming a translucent membrane of greenish tint, which contrasts with the white body. This ware is still manufactured in China and Japan.

Chia Ch'ing (1796–1820) and Tao Kuang (1821–1850)

A gradual deterioration in craftsmanship, as well as in design, had begun in the latter half of the Ch'ien Lung reign; the downward trend continued until Ch'ing-tê Chên was destroyed by the T'ai Ping rebels in 1853. During this period the painting of traditional subjects became very stilted; novel subjects were out of favor. Vases predominate; their shapes, mostly of the K'ang Hsi repertoire or borrowed from bronzes, are exaggerated, lacking both the sensitivity of Ch'ien Lung and the vitality of Yung Chêng and K'ang Hsi.

The blue is blackish and strong; the white ranges from brilliant to dead or grayish. The glaze is glassy; however, a pleasant, finely pitted glaze appears on some Chia Ch'ing pieces. A favorite border motif on Chia Ch'ing wares shows the emblems of the Eight Immortals—the fan of Chung-li Ch'uan, the gourd of Li Tieh-kuai, the flower basket of Lan Ts'ai-ho, the sword of Lü Tung-pin, the castanets of Ts'ao Kuo-ch'iu, the bamboo-tube drum and sticks of Chang-kuo Lao, the lotus of Ho Hsien-ku and the flute of Han Hsiang-tzu.

As at the end of the Ming dynasty, it is in the simple tablewares made for the domestic market that the greatest spirit is shown. Not many of these have come to light in the West, however, because Canton and Nankeen wares and enameled porcelains copying European styles satisfied the contemporary export market, and the simpler Chia Ch'ing or Tao Kuang wares have not enjoyed sufficient prestige to be sought out. But nineteenth-century vases of bronze-inspired shapes and brocade decoration are found everywhere. These often have holes drilled in the bases. As a rule the serious collector avoids pieces that are chipped, cracked or drilled.

Chia Ch'ing rice-grain bowl and cover. The Metropolitan Museum of Art, New York.

American Export Blue and White: Canton and Nankeen Wares (1790–1850)

The Willow Pattern is, no doubt, the most familiar ceramic decoration in the Western world. Though not Chinese, it is an adaptation of the landscape pictured on its early-nineteenth-century prototypes—Canton and Nankeen wares. These Chinese export porcelains both show a view of the West Lake at Hangchow in Chekiang, famous from the poetry of Su Tung-pu.

Nankeen is more carefully finished and elaborately painted than Canton, but the most tangible difference between the two wares is in their border motifs. Canton shows a simple band of blue wash over which broad criss-crosses are painted in a heavier blue; sometimes a scalloped "ruffle" is added to the inner edge of the band. Nankeen has a cleanly executed lozenge diaper border, with a spearhead border along the inner edge. Although Nankeen is usually of finer quality than Canton, there is a bit of overlapping, and a good piece of Canton may be better than a rough piece of Nankeen. Canton was made between 1790 and 1840; Nankeen dates from 1790 to 1850. Both were manufactured in Ch'ing-tê Chên. Both were purchased at Canton. But the Nankeen may have been sent by the water route from Ch'ing-tê Chên, in which case it would have been transshipped at Nanking, thus explaining its name.

The blue of these wares is, needless to say, not of the first quality. It ranges in tone from grayish lavender to a harsh sapphire. Early pieces show a hard grayish, blue or green-tinted white. A shallow dead-white appears on most later pieces. Potting is heavy, intended for rough service. Shapes show great variety, though mostly in the tableware category. There are cups, saucers, mugs, plates, hot water plates, platters, cream pitchers and sugar bowls, gravy boats, tureens (after a Wedgwood shape), bone dishes, tea, coffee, and chocolate pots; also vases, candlesticks, basket-work candy dishes and inkwells.

Canton and Nankeen are now rapidly increasing in popularity; for the most part it is well deserved. The shapes and decorations are full of humor. Pagodas on the West Lake wear their roofs like hats at a cocky angle; handles of sugar bowls seem to listen attentively. Furthermore, Canton and Nankeen rank as Americana. It was these wares that filled the deepest holds of the clipper ships and served in the dining rooms of old New England inns.

OPPOSITE: Canton pitcher. Circle represents moon reflected in the West Lake.
ABOVE: Early 15th century ewer with peony sprays surrounding cartouche containing
spray of berries. Courtesy Frank Caro, New York.

Early Korean jar with phoenix amid clouds. Museum of Fine Arts, Boston, Bequest of Charles B. Hoyt.

CHAPTER IV

Related Wares

Korean

BLUE AND WHITE WAS MANUFACTURED in Korea from the beginning of the Yi dynasty (1392); but celadon was the preferred porcelain until the end of the sixteenth century. In 1592–1598, the Japanese general, Hideyoshi, invaded Korea, devastating the country and taking many prisoners. The celadon potteries never recovered; Blue and White replaced them by default.

Korean celadon is a refined, sophisticated ware; but the Blue and White is rough, countryish porcelain; the difference reflects the plunge into poverty Korea suffered after the Japanese invasion, and not a decline of artistic sensibility. On the contrary, the Korean Blue and White displays the same affinity for powerful and imaginative shapes as the celadon, and is further enhanced by drawings of unsurpassed vigor. But the materials are of poor quality, and the working conditions were clearly primitive. Sand from the floor of the kiln often adheres to the margin of the glaze at the foot; and the porcelain body is composed of a coarse gray material full of impurities. Until 1464 imported cobalt was used, but after that year a native pigment, of harsh blue, grayish or black hue was adopted. Even the low-grade native color was expensive, and was used sparingly. Thus the drawings are simple and deft, a pleasing abstract style being developed out of necessity.

The principal potting factory in Korea was at Punwon, near Seoul. It was supported by the government until 1883, when, already failing, it passed into the hands of a private company. Ironically, the new management imported Japanese potters in an attempt to modernize production. At the beginning of the twentieth century the Yi dynasty collapsed, the Punwon factory went bankrupt, and Blue and White ceased to be made.

ABOVE: Late Korean jar decorated with a finger citron (Buddha's hand). The British Museum, London.

OPPOSITE, LEFT: Japanese *mingei* bottle with spray of chrysanthemums. Courtesy Mr. and Mrs. Fredric M. Frank.

RIGHT: Early Edo Japanese pear bottle with spray of grape vine and *ju-i* head border. Courtesy Otto Nelson.

Before Blue and White was introduced to Korea, white wares were decorated with overglaze painting in brown slip, after the style of a Chinese country ware made at Tzu Chou. It is from the heritage of this simple, rustic decoration that the style of Korean Blue and White was developed, and not from the elaborate, formalized Chinese Blue and White. Motifs of dragons passant or floral sprays appear, with either broad suggestions of border motifs or no borders at all. Their stark delineations have immediacy and grandeur.

The later wares, made under Japanese influence, show a refined white body and a more abundant use of cobalt. Painting is more elaborate and not as strong, but with a characteristic knobby brush stroke that appears self-conscious and calligraphic. Twining floral branches, medallions and finger citrons (Buddha's hands) are the favored subjects. Large jars and sturdy pear-shaped vases were the major products of the government supported factory. The later enterpreneurs favored small, intimate shapes—delicate vases, water droppers and covered bowls. Korean Blue and White was not in demand until recently, but appreciation of it is now rapidly increasing.

Japanese

The first Japanese porcelain, so tradition has it, was made by Gorodayu go Shonzui, who went to Ch'ing-tê Chên in 1510 to study potting, and returned to Japan five years later to Arita, in Hizen province, with materials to make Blue and White. But after Shonzui's materials ran out, production was discontinued. When, in 1598, General Hideyoshi brought home among his prisoners a number of Korean potters, porcelain manufacture began again. A Korean discovered deposits of petuntse near Arita at the beginning of the seventeenth century, initiating the first major phase of porcelain production in Japan. Porcelains of interest to the collector thus belong almost entirely to the Edo period (1603–1853), when Japan was ruled by the Tokugawa shogunate at Edo, the modern Tokyo.

The blue of the early-seventeenth-century Hizen wares is grayish or blackish in tone, and the white ground is distinctly gray. The effect is not unlike Korean porcelains. Drawing is restrained and masterful but shows an easy elegance which is entirely Japanese.

It was not long before Japanese potters were making imitations of Swatow and other Chinese export wares, and were receiving a few orders for pieces in European shapes and styles from the Dutch settlement at Deshima. Dutch medicine bottles, coffee urns, mustard pots, jugs and even hookah bases were made. The labels on some medicine bottles, written in underglaze blue, appear in a flowing Dutch script, suggesting that a European may have been employed in at least one of the Japanese factories.

Between 1640 and 1650 porcelain factories opened at Kutani. But overglaze enameling was the preferred technique there; and the trend spread to Arita. Blue and White continued to be made, but its styles were heavily influenced by the enameled wares, especially those of the famous Kakiemon family. The grayish paste was brightened to white. The blue remained blackish or grayish, with a lavender tinge. Brown dressing was applied to the rims of some seventeenth-century Chinese Blue and White; and the practice was adopted and retained by the Japanese.

The ideal of Japanese Blue and White was not the refined Imperial wares of Hsüan Te or Ch'êng Hua, or the heavily decorated Chia Ching wares, but the simple, whimsical export porcelain of the T'ien Ch'i reign. Borders were sparingly used; and dragons, phoenixes and lotus scrolls were avoided. Distinctly Japanese styles of painting were adapted to the ceramic surface, ranging from swiftly executed suggestions of plants or figures to carefully delineated birds, flowers, landscapes or scenes with figures. Large pieces were fired on spurs, leaving the usual little rough knobs of biscuit on the bases. Spur marks are never seen on Chinese Blue and White.

In the middle Edo period (1703–1800), the number of porcelain factories in Japan greatly increased. Two of these factories deserve special attention. The first was located at Okawichi and began production in the latter part of the seventeenth century, under the patronage of the Prince of Nabeshima. Most Nabeshima ware is decorated with enamels, but the few pieces of Blue and White are so exquisite and arresting in their originality as to mark a high point in the chart of Blue and White design. Simple plates on high conical feet are the favored form. The blue is soft and slightly lavenderish, and is applied in perfectly smooth washes or subtle blendings, with even, wirelike outlines. The white is milky or slightly grayish blue. Potting is clean and precise, albeit a little heavy. But it is the decorations that are most important; these are always surprising in their composition, and sometimes in their subject matter, though flowers and landscapes with swirls representing water predominate. The style of drawing recalls the designs on kimonos, or the great curtains of the Kabuki theater. Many modern imitations of the ware have been made.

Another factory of interest is that which was located at Mikawachi. After 1751 the workshop received the patronage of the Prince of Hirado, and the porcelain came to be known as Hirado ware. The blue is pale, with a lavender tint; the glaze is milky, but suffused with fine bubbles, softening the drawing. Draftsmanship is very delicate. Landscapes in classical styles were favored in the early manufacture, but in nineteenth-century pieces floral scrolls and other formal motifs predominate. Potting is sharp and precise. Feats of skill such as openwork and thinly supported flower petals are displayed. Some pieces have handles shaped like giant insects in full relief or ornaments dangling from porcelain chains. Small objects such as incense burners, miniature vases, boxes and brush washers, and medium- and very large-sized vases are the principal shapes. The sweetness, delicacy and novelty of Hirado made it popular in the late nineteenth century but led to some loss of favor in the twentieth.

At the beginning of the twentieth century Western methods of mass production completely superseded the old family potteries, and the making of intimate ceramics of fine quality all but came to an end. In the last few decades Japan has turned to making imitations of the heavily decorated late Ming Blue and White, especially for lamp bases. These are not mistakable for genuine Chia Ching or Wan Li however, for the blue is harsh and blackish, the white very bright and the glaze shallow and glassy. Furthermore, the painting and potting have their own peculiar assembly-line stiffness.

Of increasing interest are the peasant porcelains, *mingei,* made from the mid-seventeenth until the nineteenth century. Plates used as drip pans for oil lamps are most common, but a variety of shapes may be found. The painting is very free and full of gusto. Children and old women are said to have been employed as the decorators. A single worker was expected to finish three hundred pieces in a day, yet the drawing never shows any of the cramped dullness of mass production. The pigment is blackish to sapphire; it is a native cobalt mined near Seto and known as *sunae-gosu.* The paste is gray, sometimes with brownish, oatmeal-like speckles and gravelly impurities. The potting is roughly finished. *Mingei* are more akin in appearance to the early Japanese and Korean Blue and White than to their contemporaries. They display the same spirit and suggestiveness of design that make the older wares so attractive. Scholarly interest has lately turned to peasant wares, and a greater appreciation may be expected to follow with increasing knowledge.

Early 18th century Nabeshima plate with willow tree seen through streams of fog.
The Cleveland Museum of Art, Gift of the Twentieth Century Club.

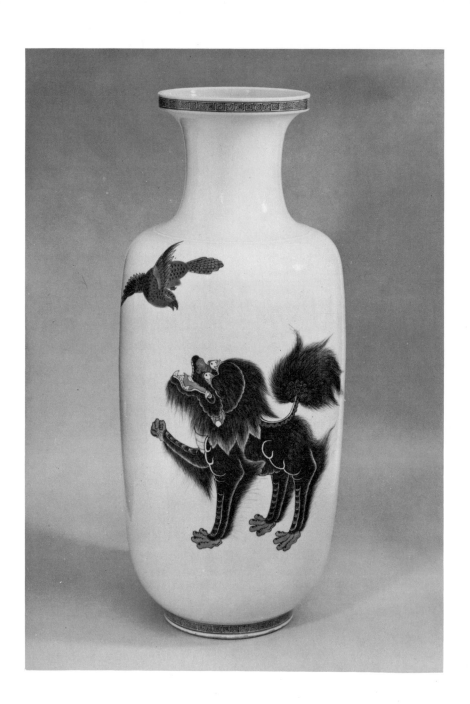

CHAPTER V

Advice for Collectors

1. See as many porcelains, genuine and fake, as possible. Touch them; become familiar with the textures of the glaze and the biscuit at the footrim.
2. Look at photographs of many pieces of each period to develop a sense of styles of decoration and potting. There are many heavily illustrated books and museum catalogs on Blue and White. Most cannot be bought at the local bookshop, but may be found in public and museum libraries. For those who want to buy their books, museum publications are generally obtainable from the museums for many years after their publication. Other books may be found in bookshops that specialize in art books, out-of-print books, and orientalia. The Ceramic Book Company (St. John's Road and Chepstow Road, Newport, Monmouthshire, England) and the Paragon Book Gallery (14 East 38th Street, New York) can be particularly helpful. And the Antiquarian Booksellers Center (630 Fifth Avenue, New York) can be very useful in locating hard-to-find books. Auctions of art books at Parke-Bernet and Swann galleries can be fruitful hunting grounds if one happens to live in New York and has free time. Obtaining books about Chinese porcelain is a serious branch of collecting too.
3. Before you shop for a porcelain have an idea of current prices. Don't be shy to ask dealers the price of objects. See what porcelains have fetched recently in important international auction houses. Selected prices are published in the quarterly *Art Prices Current,* available at any good library.

Ch'ien Lung vase finely painted with Fu dog and a bird. The Metropolitan Museum of Art, New York, Bequest of Benjamin Altman, 1913.

4. As is always the case if you are buying art as an investment, it is better to buy one costly but important piece than a dozen cheaper ones, and to buy from a reputable dealer. Such dealers are few and expensive (about double the current auction prices), but the cost of expertise runs high, and they guarantee what they sell. The recognized dealers are usually found as advertisers in responsible journals such as *Oriental Art*. When you purchase a "find" at an antique shop, you must face the possibility that the authenticity of the piece may be questioned, and your investment may be a total loss.

5. Avoid damaged or repaired pieces. A hairline crack often reduces value considerably. Also remember that the bizarre piece does not necessarily have a special virtue by its rarity, but rather is more liable to question. The piece just like a well-known object has the advantage in being familiar.

6. There is not much to be said about the care of porcelains. Their materials, being virtually impenetrable, are unaffected by atmospheric conditions. Many pieces, however, show a dark brown color on the biscuit of the footrim, which comes from the wood stain of their stands. This, and any other dirt, may be removed with a nail brush and hand soap.

7. Be a collector, not a hodgepodge accumulator. Build a collection that explores a single period or type of ware, and avoid the temptations of objects that are beautiful but have nothing to do with anything else you own.

Selected Bibliography

BLUETT, E. E. *Ming and Ch'ing Porcelain,* Privately printed, London, 1933.

BRANKSTON, A. D. *Ming Wares of Chingtechen,* Henri Vetch, Peking, 1938.

BUSHELL, S. W. *Description of Chinese Pottery and Porcelain, being a translation of the T'ao Shuo,* The Clarendon Press, Oxford, 1910.

———. *Oriental Ceramic Art,* text edition, D. Appleton and Co., New York, 1899.

CROSSMAN, CARL L. *A Design Catalogue of Chinese Export Porcelain for the American Market,* Peabody Museum, Salem, Mass., 1964.

FOX, ROBERT. *The Catalagan Excavations: Two 15th Century Burial Sites in Batangas, Philippines,* Manila, 1959.

GARNER, SIR HARRY. *Oriental Blue and White,* Faber and Faber, London, 1954.

JENYNS, S. *Later Chinese Porcelain,* Thomas Yoseloff, New York, 1965.

————. *Ming Pottery and Porcelain,* Faber and Faber, London, 1953.

KIM, DR. CHEWON, and G. ST. G. M. GOMPERTZ. *The Ceramic Art of Korea,* Faber and Faber, London, 1961.

KOYAMA, FUJIO. *Japanese Ceramics from Ancient to Modern Times,* The Oakland Art Museum, 1961.

LEE, JEAN GORDON. *Ming Blue and White,* Philadelphia Museum Bulletin, Vol. XLIV, No. 233, Autumn, 1949.

MEDLEY, MARGARET. *Illustrated Catalogue of Porcelains Decorated in Underglaze Blue and Copper Red in the Percival David Foundation of Chinese Art,* University of London, London, 1963.

MUNSTERBERG, HUGO. *Folk Arts of Old Japan,* Asia House, New York, 1965.

NATIONAL PALACE MUSEUM. *Porcelains of the National Palace Museum,* Vol. 4, Books 1–6, Taiwan, n.d.

ORIENTAL CERAMIC SOCIETY. *Catalogue of an Exhibition of Chinese Blue and White, 14th to 19th Centuries,* The Oriental Ceramic Society, London, 1953.

POPE, JOHN ALEXANDER. *Chinese Porcelains from the Ardebil Shrine,* Smithsonian Institution, Freer Gallery of Art, Washington, D.C., 1956.

————. *Fourteenth Century Blue and White, A Group of Chinese Porcelains in the Topkapu Sarayi Müzesi, Istanbul,* Freer Gallery of Art Occasional Papers, Washington, D.C., 1952.

————. *Ming Porcelains in the Freer Gallery of Art,* Smithsonian Institution, Washington, D.C., 1953.

SAYER, GEOFFREY. *Ching-tê-chên T'ao-lu,* Routledge and Kegan Paul, London, 1951.

VOLKER, T. *The Japanese Porcelain Trade of the Dutch East India Company after 1683,* Leiden, 1959.

————. *Porcelain and the Dutch East India Company, 1620–1682,* Leiden, 1954.

WIRGIN, JAN. *Blavitt Ming-Porslin: Ming Blue and White,* Museum of Far Eastern Antiquities Catalogue no. 1, Stockholm, 1964.

PERIODICALS

AGA-OGLU, KAMER. "Ming Export Blue and White Jars in the University of Michigan Collection," *Art Quarterly,* No. 11, 1948, Detroit.

AYERS, JOHN. "Early Chinese Blue and White in the Museum of Eastern Art, Oxford," *Oriental Art,* No. 3, 1951, London.

FERRIS, ALICE M. "17th Century Transitional Porcelains," *Oriental Art,* No. 3, 1968, London.

LEE, JEAN GORDON. "Some Pre-Ming Blue and White, a Stylistic Analysis with Suggested Chronology," *Archives,* of the Chinese Art Society of America, No. 6, 1952, New York.

POPE, JOHN A. "Blue and White in London," *Far Eastern Ceramics Bulletin,* No. 269-14, June, 1954, Ann Arbor.

————. "Ming Blue and White at Philadelphia," *Oriental Art,* No. 3, 1950, London.

REITLINGER, GERALD, and M. BUTTON. "Early Ming Blue and White," *Burlington Magazine,* January and March, 1948, London.

Early 15th century plate with foliate rim; borders of crapemyrtle scroll and floral sprays; central motif of grapes. Courtesy Frank Caro, New York.